Holoplexity:
Theory of Consciousness

Holoplexity:
Theory of Consciousness

Adam M. Sturdevant

INARA PUBLISHING

AN IMPRINT OF GCRR PRESS
1312 17TH STREET SUITE 549
DENVER, CO 80202

INFO@GCRR.ORG • INARAPUBLISHING.COM

Inara Publishing
An imprint of GCRR Press
1312 17th Street Suite 549
Denver, CO 80202
www.inarapublishing.com

DOI: 10.33929/GCRRPress.2022.06

Typesetter/Copyeditor: Fox Raud
Proofreader: Alexandra Hademenos
Cover Design: Abdullah Al Mahmud
                fiverr.com/mahmuddidar

Library of Congress Cataloging-in-Publication Data

Holoplexity : theory of consciousness / Adam M. Sturdevant
p.   cm.
Includes bibliographic references (p.).
ISBN (Print): 978-1-959281-04-7
ISBN (eBook): 978-1-959281-05-4
1. Consciousness.   2. Mind and body.   3. Thought and thinking.
4. Phenomenological psychology.   I. Title.

B808.9.S78   2022

೫

This book is dedicated to my loving wife Joanne,
without whom this book would still only be an idea.

Advanced Endorsement

Be prepared for a phantasmagorical journey into the realm of consciousness. Dr. Sturdevant's unique theory of consciousness, which he has termed "Holoplexity Theory," was designed to provide tentative answers to some of the long-standing questions posed in the literature on consciousness. His theory combines existing theories and previous conceptual understandings with additions based, not only on what has been conceptualized before but also, and most importantly, on his own formulation that builds on these other notable theories. His remarkable thesis sparked my interest in this fascinating philosophical question that is also immensely germane to the field of psychology.

–Ann-Marie Neale, PhD
Karen Horney Professor of Counseling and Psychology
Graduate Theological Foundation

Contents

1   Introduction   1

2   Literature Review   27

3   Methodology   48

4   Findings   60

5   Analysis and Synthesis   78

6   Conclusions, Recommendations and Limitations   123

8   References   138

Index   153

Introduction

This study began as a sincere attempt to answer, "the hard problem of consciousness" (Chalmers, 1996) by the researcher, in a physiological psychology course in graduate school in 2008. The pursuit of a *reasonable account* to answer this question continued as a kind of very enjoyable hobby or avocation for the researcher. In the pursuit of the answers to the many, many sub-questions that popped up, again and again, the researcher found he began to collect *personally satisfactory* answers to many of the numerous sub-questions. Eventually, the author began to see that there was just as much confusion within the literature, as there was a coherent body of information, among the many competing and complementary theories of consciousness.

As the information began to point toward a specific conceptualization of consciousness that the researcher personally held; the researcher decided to add a bit of discipline and structure into this pursuit to determine whether or not it might add up to a *coherent, original account of consciousness* sufficient to answer many of the questions in the literature, but especially the hard problem of consciousness. This dissertation is the result of those thirteen years of pursuing such an account.

To begin: What *exactly* is consciousness? Is it *synonymous with* or *separate from* human consciousness? The nature of human consciousness has been a philosophical and scientific mystery of the ages. From before Descartes' day to today, it continues to be regarded as an elusive mystery. Some thinkers sincerely believe that this mystery will be solved someday, eventually. Others believe that human beings can never truly understand consciousness due to inherent human cognitive and perceptual limitations. Which is it?

Consciousness, as a term, connotes several things to most people and holds specifically denoted separate and distinct meanings within various disciplines of study. Because language is arguably the primary vehicle of transferring knowledge, the confusion and imprecision of language is a serious barrier. Consider that the expression "acting consciously" means acting with awareness of one's intent, whereas "being conscious" means being aware and acting with one's faculties, and "acting with social consciousness" means being aware of social responsibility and acting in accord. Consider also that the meaning of the word "unconscious" in sleep science differs from the word "unconscious" within psychotherapy. The imprecision and overuse of the term "conscious" both tend to contribute to a general and ongoing confusion of the meaning within the study of consciousness today.

Today, as mentioned, there is no agreed-upon definition for the term *consciousness*. Does it emerge from the human mind? How does it emerge from the human mind if so? What is this idea of *emergence* exactly? Is the consciousness that human beings experience qualitatively different than consciousness itself? Is there a separation of "consciousness itself" from "human consciousness"? Is consciousness a physical phenomenon, such as space? What is the relationship of consciousness to the idea of time? Could consciousness be even *more basic* than time and space? Perhaps time, space, and consciousness itself are aspects of the same thing? If so, how could this be? And even if it is the same as time and space—what does that have to do with the consciousness that we experience as human beings? Perhaps everything, or maybe perhaps nothing. This study is first an examination of the existing contemporary conceptual findings and theories, and second the building of an *alternative conceptual explanation in principle* for what is known. The new theory combines existing theory with the conceptual creations and additions of the author.

The resultant theory is designed to provide one possible alternative understanding in principle and to provide tentative answers to some of the long-standing questions posed in the literature of consciousness. The term "theory" here is used to denote a coherent system of explanatory hypotheses concerning a particular phenomenon (Reber, Allen & Reber, 2009).

Why put time and energy into yet another theory of consciousness? Is there not an adequate number of these theories already? As the Australian philosopher David Chalmers (1997) somewhat humorously noted:

> Researchers working on the easy problems already outnumber those working on the hard problem by at least a hundred to one, so there is not much danger of the world suddenly falling into unproductive navel-gazing.... Granted that the hard problem is hard, it nevertheless seems quite reasonable for a community to invest a fraction of its resources into trying to solve it. After all, we do not know when a solution will come. Even if we do not solve it immediately, it may well be part of that understanding that comes through searching for a solution that will help us in the future search, in our work on the easy problems, and our understanding of ourselves. *It is in the scientific spirit to try.* (p. 12, emphasis added)

This is where this journey began, and this dissertation and theory are the results of that quest. The author agreed wholeheartedly with this sentiment when it was first put forth. In past scientific developments, once a scientific mystery was identified, *the question itself was opened to all attempts to solve that mystery!* The keyword here is the word *all.* When what has been achieved previously, as specific to mechanistic-style thinking, has provided no solution thus far, it only makes sense then to look for viable answers in places *other than the usual places.*

For the author, the search for the answer here may be likened to a common but exhaustive search for *lost keys.* The search for lost keys is *first* conducted where they are thought they *should be.* However, if that provides no solution, should the search be discontinued? Of course not! The search for the *lost keys* continues in less likely and more uncommon places! This is a parallel situation to the search for the answers to the "hard problem of consciousness" (Chalmers, 1996). We must now continue to look in less likely and more uncommon places for answers. Admittedly, the theory contained in this work constitutes a metaphorically *less likely place.* This theory contains concepts and ideas not found within other theories—which is why it is considered *less likely.* It might also be why this particular theory provides potential answers to questions that most other theories do not. If correct (or simply *more correct*), this theory may provide a framework for a greater understanding of what consciousness may ultimately turn out to be. Again, it is in the *scientific spirit* that this theory is offered.

Background

The scientific history of consciousness began as a tenuous one, paralleling and often considered interchangeable with the histories of the brain, neurophysiology, and psychology (Blackmore, 2004; Carter, Aldridge, Page & Parker, 2014; Revonsuo, 2010). In this work, *consciousness* is used in a general way. *Consciousness itself* is used as a technical term to denote the *stuff* of what consciousness eventually turns out to be. The term *human consciousness* is used to denote the human experience of consciousness.

The systematic history of *consciousness itself* arguably began with philosopher René Descartes (1596-1650), as the founder of dualism. Arguably, Descartes made the basic distinction between *consciousness itself* and *human consciousness*. This is reflected within the *basic* dichotomy in the literature as monism versus dualism. Generally, *monism* is broadly defined as the world and all reality itself consisting of a singular substance. Descartes' dualism was defined as a dichotomy between the physical and the mental. This conceptual dichotomy was determined to be useful initially within this study but was later determined to be too broad to be useful as it later appeared that consciousness may be expressed *both* monistically and dualistically, depending upon which level it was examined. Given the complexity of what consciousness was hypothesized to be and given that *consciousness itself* as a separate category was not established, it then makes sense that the literature would reflect its state of incompleteness and its relative confusion.

Interestingly, despite all the technological advances of modern scientific inquiry, the Ancients seemed to have already established and occupied many important philosophical positions in the modern-day consciousness debate (Edelman & Tononi, 2000; Frith & Rees, 2017). For example, Baruch Spinoza (1632-1677) proposed that the mental and physical were different aspects of the same singular substance, consistent with the current notion of dual-aspect theory (Carruthers, 2017; Chalmers, 1996, 2017; Tononi, 2004, 2017). Gottfried Leibniz (1646-1716) hypothesized that mental and physical were composed of different things, but that they were structured to run together harmoniously, consistent with today's notion of psychophysical parallelism (Eccles, 1994). However, Emmanuel Kant (1724-1804) rigidly denied that mathematics and experimentation (thought to be the cornerstones of science) applied to descriptions of mental phenomena as they only vary in the single dimension of time, therefore denying consciousness as a scientific subject.

Several existing theories examined were too specific in scope, or too circumscribed by explanation, to be specifically useful to the search for the human experience of consciousness or for consciousness itself (Carruthers, 2017; Hameroff & Penrose, 1996; Lamme, 2006; Prinz, 2017; Seager & Bourget, 2017; Strawson, 2017; Varela, 1995; Zeki, 1999). Some theories were excluded based on a single factor or multiple criteria. However, many components of theories still are included partially within the findings (Carruthers, 2017; Eccles, 1994; Strawson, 2017). What was very relevant here was the distinction between the *hard* and the *easy* problems of consciousness, as delineated by Chalmers (2017b). Excluded were the theories that tended to focus on the "easy problems" (Chalmers, 2017b, p. 364) of consciousness which included these several criteria: (1) the ability to discriminate, categorize, and react to environmental stimuli; (2) the integration of information by a cognitive system; (3) the reportability of mental states; (4) the ability of a system to access its internal states; (5) the focus of attention; (6) the deliberate control of behavior; and (7) the difference between wakefulness and sleep.

It should be noted that some aspects of these defined *easy problems* are indicative of how human beings "experience consciousness" in contradistinction to how human beings "apprehend" consciousness itself. This fine distinction alone contributes to and accounts for some of the confusion as seen within the literature. It turns out that the complexity of consciousness cannot be easily or adequately captured by a simple dichotomy—it is far richer and more complex than that. We all know about levels of complexity, but we do not typically find such deep rich complexity in our everyday lives. Interestingly, most of the theories that were deemed "not useful" for this study were both very useful and seemingly correct at many different other levels of complexity.

The search for a viable answer to the hard problem of consciousness began within the human brain, but quickly led outside the brain and eventually to the origins of the universe and reality at its most basic level (but the perhaps most complex level to conceptualize) of understanding. Some concepts are more clearly developed, and so conceptualizations to aid understanding were borrowed from the fields of chemistry, biology, and physics in this pursuit of a coherent account.

Consciousness itself as a distinct, separate substance or phenomenon was expressly limited or *denied* by some theories and theorists on various empirical or scientific bases (Crick & Koch, 1990; Damasio, 1996, 1999; Edelman & Tononi, 2000; Koch & Crick, 1994; Llinas, 2002; Searle, 1993, 2000, 2017). Koch (neurobiological theory), regarding consciousness in a published interview, clearly stated that he believed subjectivity was out of the purview of science (Koch, 1992). Damasio (somatic marker theory) admits his skepticism that science will solve the hard problem of consciousness and purposefully delimits his theory to reflect this. Edelman and Tononi (dynamic core theory) state that they do not believe consciousness is an object, but rather a process. Llinas (thalamocortical binding theory) explained that he does not believe consciousness exists outside the realm of the nervous system function. Like Llinas, Searle (biological naturalism) advocated for a kind of limited consciousness but denied its existence outside of being a *product of* the human mind.

Consciousness itself and human consciousness were variously denied by some theories and theorists as reduced, re-identified, re-labeled, or re-named consciousness as something else (Hameroff & Penrose, 1996; Seager & Bourget, 2017; O'Regan & Noe, 2001; Varela, 1995; Zeki, 1999). Most quantum theories were generally limited to theories of mental *causality* in which the attributes of quantum mechanics were thought to contribute; as such, they were generally restricted to functionally focused theories which did not tend to address the hard problem of consciousness. Modern representationalism theory by Seager and Bourget was found to be more of an *approach* to information processing within the brain, than a full-blown theory of consciousness; thus, it was far too narrow in scope to answer the broader question of how information becomes an experience and/or its relationship to consciousness. O'Regan and Noe (sensorimotor theory) do not deny consciousness but limit their theory of it to *awareness* of the interaction of the body with environment. Varela (neurophenomenology theory) realized and emphasized the primacy of consciousness but limited his theory to the empirical/methodological issues associated with the first-person perspective as within a third-person dominant scientific paradigm. Zeki's microconsciousness theory is an interesting discovery, one that may turn out to be objectively verifiable, but as written it offers little to the greater understanding of the larger, overall hard problem of consciousness.

Consciousness itself as exclusively human consciousness was denied by some theories and theorists and thus reduced to a kind of mere *functionalism* (Dretske, 2012; Lamme, 2006; Lehar, 2003; Metzinger, 2009; Prinz, 2017; Rosenthal, 2012; Vision, 2017). Dretske and Rosenthal are higher-order awareness (HOA) theorists who believed that consciousness could be explained by the interactive function of a higher-order state over a lower-order state. Lamme (recurrent processing theory) reduced consciousness to mere neural functioning. Lehar and Metzinger are virtual reality (VR) theorists; VR theories tend to limit consciousness to the confines of the brain. Prinz (intermediate level theory) was overly focused on the exact location of where human consciousness may materialize while merely presuming the existence of consciousness itself and giving it no further thought. Vision (emergentism theory) created a new category for consciousness as emergent from neuronal interaction, while not adequately addressing how this might occur.

Consciousness was even denied outright as illusory by some authors (Dennett, 1991; Rosenthal, 2004, 2012). Philosopher Daniel Dennett (multiple drafts theory) famously *explained-away* consciousness in his book *Consciousness Explained* (1991) by asserting that there exists a kind of *fame in the brain* in which one draft of information takes primacy over other competing drafts, rather than conceptualizing human consciousness as an independent phenomenon. In 2004, Rosenthal (an HOA theorist) joined Dennett in concluding that phenomenal human consciousness was illusory.

There are a handful of theorists that do not deny the existence of consciousness (Baars, 2005; Bohm, 1980; Carruthers, 2017; Chalmers, 1995, 2017b; Dehaene, 2014; Strawson, 2017; Tononi, 2004; Velmans, 1990, 2008, 2017a). Baars' and Dehaene's theories (global workspace theorists) both begin and end with observable phenomena in the brain and that the hard problem did not apply. However, this was not viewed as a denial of the existence of consciousness, but rather a reflection of the *limitation of methods* as well as the fact that Baars and Dehaene were concerned with *human consciousness* and not its nexus with *consciousness itself.* Bohm (implicate order theory), while technically a quantum theorist, did not limit his theorizing to mental causality, but instead espoused a rich, deep theory that began with an ontological interpretation of quantum reality (*as consciousness itself*) and extended to human consciousness and cognition. Like Baars and Dehaene, Carruthers (dual-content theory) had a similarly circumscribed account that did not include consciousness itself, but rather a kind of human consciousness that suggested larger aspects of consciousness by dual qualities. Chalmers (naturalistic dualism theory) admitted that his theory had at least one *missing* nonreductive *extra ingredient* toward an explanation of consciousness, although Chalmers was able to provide a general description of the missing extra ingredient. Strawson's (physicalist panpsychism) theory limits its focus on "consciousness itself" rather than an expanded theory of consciousness itself including human consciousness. Tononi's (information integration) theory is a mathematical description of experience and is already formatted in the dual-aspect format of the information *bit*. Velmans' theory was a reformulation of an ancient monistic theory (reflexive monism) which posits consciousness itself as being much more pervasive than commonly thought.

Problem Statement

"We know that a theory of consciousness requires the addition of something fundamental to our ontology, as everything in physical theory is compatible with the absence of consciousness" (Chalmers,

2017, p. 364). Chalmers chose to eliminate the "easy problems" of consciousness because he felt that they availed themselves to ordinary, current methods of scientific inquiry. The "easy problems" then will be defined by those problems which avail themselves to current scientific methods. These easy problems of consciousness were *not* the subject of this study. However, as these are interacting systems, some understanding of some processes involved in the easy problems of consciousness may tend to make explicit some aspects of the hard problem. Reformulated in the words of the author: How does *consciousness itself* become *human consciousness*?

The Hard Problem of Consciousness

Chalmers (2005; 2017a) gave an additional overview of what he considered was missing from the study of consciousness. Chalmers (2017a, p. 39) cited the need for an "extra ingredient" that did not exist among the current leading theories of consciousness. Chalmers (2017a) elaborated further, stating:

> Why doesn't all this information processing go on "in the dark," free of any inner feel? Why is it that when electromagnetic waveforms impinge on a retina and are discriminated against and categorized by a visual system, this discrimination and categorization are experienced as a sensation of vivid red? We know that conscious experience does arise when these functions are performed, but the very fact that it arises is the central mystery. There is an explanatory gap (a term due to Levine 1983) between the functions and experience, and we need an explanatory bridge to cross it. A mere account of the functions stays on one side of the gap, so the materials of the bridge must be found elsewhere. (p. 35)

However, the author feels that the key to finding the right answers to missing information is asking the right (or at least different) questions. As necessary, the questions inherent in the hard problem of consciousness will be recursively re-interpreted as the data tends to indicate.

Experience as Fundamental

Chalmers began his study of consciousness by hypothesizing that experience is fundamental. Chalmers (2017b) stated:

> Of course, by taking experience as fundamental, there is a sense in which this approach does not tell us why there is experience in the first place. But this is the same for any fundamental theory. Nothing in physics tells us why there is matter in the first place, but we do not count this against theories of matter. Certain features of the world need to be taken as fundamental by any scientific theory. A theory of matter can still explain all sorts of facts about matter, by showing how they are consequences of the basic laws. The same goes for a theory of experience. (p. 364) Chalmers (2017a) further added, "The hard problem of consciousness is the problem of experience. When we think and perceive, there is a whir of information-processing, but there is also a subjective aspect (p. 33)."

Chalmers essentially reformulated the hard problem consciousness. The question as reformulated by Chalmers is: *How does information become experience?*

Theoretical Framework

The following is a *general prescription* by Chalmers (2005, 2017b) for an adequate theory of consciousness. As such, it constitutes this book's *general theoretical framework.* Chalmers (2005, 2017b) laid out the criteria for a more adequate theory of consciousness: (1) It must be nonreductive; (2) it may contain "The Double-Aspect Theory of Information" (p. 370); (3) it retains [an] element(s) of speculation not present in other theories; (4) it must possess "organizational invariance" (p. 368); (5) it must be compatible with the data we have; (6) it possesses "structural coherence" (p. 365); (7) it postulates experience as fundamental; and (8) it should be simple and elegant.

Research Question

Does enough data exist in literature upon which to predicate an original, empirically compatible, nonreductive theory of consciousness sufficient to answer the hard problem of consciousness?

Hypothesis

Sufficient data exists within the literature to predicate an original, empirically compatible, nonreductive theory of consciousness that is sufficient to answer the hard problem of consciousness.

Purpose of Work

The purpose of this work is the generation of an original, empirically compatible, nonreductive theory of consciousness that offers a viable answer to the hard problem of consciousness.

Overview of Methodology

Grounded Theory Methodology

Grounded theory is the methodology of choice for this *type* of study because the outcome desired is a *new* theory generated from *existing* theory. Grounded theory is a *theory discovery methodology* (Martin & Turner, 1986). Grounded theory was the appropriate methodology for this work as the goal was the generation of new theory.

This qualitative study was undertaken by applying the tenets of ground theory's systematic methodology. Grounded theory as a design is a systematic, qualitative procedure used to generate new theory, which in turn explains a process, an action, or an interaction about a substantive topic at a broad conceptual level (Creswell, 2008). Grounded theory refers to an inductive, general method used to build new theory.

The new theory created by this approach was recursively tied back to additional existing data, such that the resultant theory was consistent with some specific aspects of existing data. The purpose of this study was to not only generate a new theory but also to show clearly how the newly created novel theory related conceptually to existing theory, and to include how some specific aspects were surmised from specific existing theory (*transparency*).

This work uses a qualitative constant comparative analysis *search* for the existing building blocks of what was known about consciousness to lay the foundation of the building of this newly proposed theory. Grounded theory's methods of synthesis and abduction, a new theory was generated, which is proposed as an *original*, empirically compatible, nonreductive theory of consciousness that is believed to be sufficient to attempt to answer the hard problem of consciousness.

The researcher examined and reviewed the existing data then used that data to ground *and* develop the proposed theory. This proposed theory is *grounded* in the data; therefore, it is conceptually well-supported at nearly all levels of development. Consequently, the proposed theory tends to provide answers to several questions posed in the literature. This theory offered an answer to *the hard problem of consciousness*.

Rationale and Significance

The central question of the hard problem of consciousness was thoroughly outlined by Chalmers (1996; 2017a; 2017b). As the framer of this central question, it seemed appropriate and consistent to use Chalmers' own words to illustrate. The researcher's rationale and significance of *this* study are the same as Chalmers'.

Chalmers, in 2017, stated in an interview that consciousness was the key to our sense of *meaning*, "What gives life even the potential for meaning in the first place is, I guess, consciousness. It takes somehow all this activity in the brain or body and turns it into meaning, like water into wine" (Horgan, 2017).

Definitions of Key Terminology

Abduction

Abduction, according to Birks and Mills (2015), is a kind of logical reasoning that begins with an examination of the relevant data and the subsequent formulation of hypotheses. These hypotheses are then either proved or disproved during the process of analysis and thereby aiding in the conceptualization of further theorizing. An example of abductive reasoning is, "because 2-D information gives rise to 3-D information and because it appears to be enabled by the juxtaposition of information, that the 3-D information must be contained within the 2-D information itself."

Advanced Coding

Advanced coding, according to Birks and Mills (2015), is defined as a technique that is used for the facilitation of integration for a final grounded theory. In this work, an example of advanced coding is the generalizing of the concept contained in the notion of "dual-aspect" from various theories under various differing labels.

Amygdala

Amygdala, according to Carter (2014), is an almond-shaped structure that is a part of the brain's limbic system; the amygdala "tastes" (p. 127) all incoming stimuli and signals other areas to produce appropriate emotional responses. It is proposed that the amygdala is also one site in which the concept of self is embedded into incoming stimuli.

In this work, certain stimuli, including internally generated thoughts, are thought to cause a change in the body by activating the limbic system, especially the amygdala. In holoplexity theory, it is the amygdala, rather than the hippocampus, that is the predominant purveyor of stimuli and creator of memories as the hippocampus is not mature until about thirty months of age. The amygdala is an important part of the hypothesized temporary sentience acquisition system (TSAS).

Autopoiesis

Autopoiesis refers to a central tenet of the Santiago theory of cognition. Autopoiesis, a term coined by Maturana and Varela in the 1970s, comes from two roots: first is "auto" which means "self" and refers to the autonomy of self-organizing systems, and secondly, "poiesis" which is also the Greek root word for "poetry" means "making" in this context; thus the term autopoiesis means "self-making." In this study, an autopoietic system, such as the mind, undergoes continual structural changes while preserving its pattern of organization, or identity. An example of this is "learning."

Binding Problem

The binding problem is a problem related to human consciousness, first recognized by Treisman (1980), about the question of how the background, objects, and emotional features are combined and experienced as a single experience. In this study, an example of this is found within the work of Treisman (1980) and Tye (2017). The *binding problem* is not a focus of this study, but it is a substantive code, and therefore useful in demarcating the boundaries to some of the easy problems of consciousness from the hard one.

Concept of Self

The concept of self (hereafter known as COS) is sentience as a self-referential neurocognitive construct that is combined with ongoing human consciousness and awareness activities which then generates the neurocognitive concept of self. In this study, the COS is integral and appears to be the point at which, upon apprehension by the COS, *consciousness itself* becomes *human consciousness*.

Consciousness Itself

Consciousness itself is used as a technical term here. It refers to the hypothetical irreducible singularity from which *all else* in the universe is comprised. In this study, it is recognized as distinct from human consciousness and further hypothesized to be the most basic underlying construct of the universe and reality as we know it.

Central Organizing Mechanism

The central organizing mechanism, or COM, is the concept of self (COS) which is hypothesized to become a neurocognitive code and embedded within each memory created, becoming retrievable by virtue of that code, and thereby thought to become the central organizing principle of the brain and mind. In this theory, the COS becomes the central organizing mechanism (COM). This may result in confusion for the human as the *experiencer* because humans tend to attribute "consciousness as experienced" as "internally generated", instead of "merely apprehended" internally.

Dimension

Dimension as a term in this study is used, first classically, to refer to the commonly known dimensions of 3-D and secondly to refer to the non-spatial features of the hypothetical irreducible singularity of consciousness itself from which *all else* in the universe is comprised. In this study, dimension is used as a broad term. Nothing in holoplexity theory suggests that anything about classical physics or any other branch of science is not as it appears to be. Rather, this is a broad re-conceptualization of the underlying foundation of our most basic assumptions.

Evidence

Evidence refers to research outcomes that tend to lend support to the existence of a concept, construct, phenomenon, or theory. In this study, concepts contained in established and generally accepted alternative theories are considered *evidence*, not necessarily of truth, but of the viability of a specific concept. An example is again that 3-D information appears to be derived from juxtaposed 2-D information. This concept is very well-established in the literature, and thus may be taken as *evidence* that the 3-D information inheres in its 2-D manifestation.

Easy Problems of Consciousness

Easy Problems of Consciousness refers to those questions associated with the study of consciousness which avail themselves to the current methods of scientific inquiry. In this study, the easy problems of consciousness delimit the parameters of the hard problem of consciousness. For example, once the temporary sentience acquisition system (TSAS) and the concept of self (COS) are hypothesized to apprehend electromagnetic manifestations of consciousness itself, those manifestations become human consciousness and a human experience—then after that point in the process, they become the easy problems of consciousness—because human consciousness after this point can be studied via the current scientific methods of inquiry.

Electromagnetism

Electromagnetism refers to the study of electromagnetic force, a type of physical interaction that occurs between electrically charged particles. Electromagnetic force is one of the four fundamental forces and expresses electromagnetic fields such as magnetic fields, electric fields, and light. In this work, electromagnetism is hypothesized to have a dual aspect with consciousness itself and to be highly compatible with other manifestations of itself.

Emergentism

Emergentism refers to the notion that consciousness and conscious states arise from ingredients that are not themselves conscious. This study rejects emergentism as a viable explanatory theory of human consciousness because it tends to implicitly deny the ontology of human consciousness and necessarily consciousness itself. The idea of emergence creates a category and places *emergent consciousness* in it. However, it fails to explain how consciousness arises from non-conscious foundations.

Epiphenomenalism

Epiphenomenalism refers to the idea that mental events are caused by physical events in the brain but have no effect in the physical world. In this study, this is a very complicated problem that is found in parallel to the hard problem of consciousness. It is often used by some theorists to relegate human consciousness to a superfluous byproduct of the brain. Relegating human consciousness to the status of a mere "byproduct" eliminates the hard problem of consciousness and explains the lack of an adequate theory to answer the question(s) associated with the hard problem of consciousness.

Epistemology

Epistemology is a subdiscipline of philosophy that is concerned with the study of knowledge. In this study, epistemology is solely concerned with what human beings can know about the nature of consciousness. Is the nature of consciousness even knowable?

Explanatory Gap

The explanatory gap is a descriptive term coined by Levine (1983) used concerning the hard problem of consciousness to denote the discrepancy between brain *functions* and our *experience* as humans. In this work, the explanatory gap is conceptualized as a substantive code and, as such, was useful in demarcating both the distinctions between the easy problems of consciousness and the hard problem of consciousness and the distinction between human consciousness and consciousness itself.

Extra Ingredient

The extra ingredient is a term coined by Chalmers (1996) that refers to the theoretical inadequacy of current theories to address the hard problem of consciousness without reducing, renaming, or denying human consciousness. Chalmers hypothesizes that there is at least one missing "extra ingredient" necessary to create an adequate theory of (human) consciousness. This suspicion by Chalmers is echoed in other languages, throughout the consciousness literature in other theories by various other authors cited in this work.

Hard Problem of Consciousness

The hard problem of consciousness is a term introduced by David Chalmers (1996) to describe the difficulty in explaining "dualism" also known previously as the "mind/body problem". In this work, the hard problem of consciousness is conceptualized, as interpreted by Chalmers (1995), as the question of *how does information become experience?*

Hippocampus

The hippocampus is a seahorse-shaped structure that is a part of the brain's limbic system. The key role of the hippocampus is the creation and retrieval of memories. It is important to note however that the hippocampus is not mature until the age of about two and a half years.

In this work, the hippocampus is involved in making personal or episodic memories, which may include an emotional component. Consequently, when these memories are retrieved, it creates a *reexperiencing* of these past emotions which may be mixed with current emotions. This is thought to partially account for why an experience has a *feel*. The hippocampus is also one site in which it is proposed that the COS is embedded into incoming stimuli.

Holoplexity

Holoplexity is a term coined by the author. It is used as a descriptive term. The term is a combination of two root words, "whole" or "holistic" as designated by the term *holo-*; and "complexity" or "multiplicity" which is denoted by the term *-plexity*. The term holoplexity was coined by the author to convey the idea of everything as originating from a single source or a single thing.

Human Consciousness

Human consciousness throughout this work specifically refers to the cognitive awareness that human beings possess by virtue of their brains. In this work, human consciousness is specifically proposed to be distinct from consciousness itself.

In Vivo Codes

In vivo codes refer to the verbatim words or phrases found within the data, which are used to communicate a broader concept that is also contained in the data. In this work, in vivo codes are often direct quotes and terms coined by their authors to indicate a specific phenomenon, problem, or concept. Examples of in vivo codes are "the hard problem of consciousness" and the "explanatory gap." Such codes refer to conceptualizations of problems that exist within the general study of consciousness.

Induction

Induction, according to Birks and Mills (2015), refers to a kind of reasoning which begins with a broader range of concepts that are then "collapsed and integrated" (p. 179) in the process of conducting research. In this work, abductive reasoning is a kind of induction, and both kinds of reasoning amplify premises into generalizations. An example in this work is the proposition that consciousness itself predates the universe since the universe is presumed to exist in time, in addition to having begun with the Big Bang.

Neurocognitive

Neurocognitive refers to both cognitive functioning and the brain structures associated with those processes. In this study, this is an important concept because there is thought to be no real separation between the two. An example is the neurocognitive concept of self. Recalling that it is postulated that there was a time in development in which human beings do not possess the neurocognitive COS, it typically develops with the assistance of the hypothesized temporary sentience acquisition system (TSAS). This neurocognitive "code" becomes the possession of the brain and of itself. Further, the neurocognitive code becomes embedded into incoming stimuli streams, thus becoming a part of all memories created.

Nonlocality

Nonlocality is typically a quantum physics term and refers to action at a distance. This is in contrast with locality, which means an object can only be influenced by something immediately next to it. In this study, nonlocality is thought to explain "perceptual projection" as a phenomenon, as perhaps the clearest example.

Ontology

Ontology is a metaphysical term that refers to the study of being and existence. In this work, it is the central question behind the concept of consciousness itself. Does it exist as a thing unto itself?

Panpsychism

Panpsychism, according to Revonsuo (2010), is the philosophical theory in which consciousness inheres in all things and all places. In this work, panpsychism is the central, prevailing theory. Holoplexity theory is predicated on this basic philosophical premise but goes a step further in order to propose that *all* things are comprised of consciousness itself, as differentiated and manifest, including three sub-dimensions that humans conceive of as 3-D.

Perceptual Projection

The mystery of *perceptual projection* refers to the question and notion of how proximal neural causes within the brain support experienced events that seem to be outside the brain. This work proposes that human brains are thought to be influenced by the larger timeless dimension of consciousness itself, which is further thought to reside *between* one moment and the next (*effectively hidden*, as humans are proposed to exist in the aftereffect only, and we possess only a *memory* of the previous moment).

Quantum Theory

Quantum, in physics, refers to the minimum amount of any physical entity that is involved in an interaction; *Quantum theory*, in physics, refers to the theoretical understanding that explains the nature and behavior of matter and energy on the most basic levels of existence. The search for an adequate theory to address the hard problem of consciousness led the author to the most basic level of existence, which is hypothesized to be isomorphic with quantum mechanics.

Recursive

Recursive here refers to relating to the repeated application of a concept or set of procedures, to a successive result. In this work, in grounded theory, it is the continuous changing of the viability of concepts as new information and new concepts become understood by the author.

Reflexive

Reflexive refers to something always referring back to itself, such as the person referring to himself or herself. In this work, this concept is integral to understanding the reflexive monism theory by Velmans (1990), which is a parallel view of the universe as holoplexity theory. Velmans developed his theory to reconcile the schism between the subject and the object within science. However, broken down into its component parts, it states essentially the same thing that holoplexity theory does—that all comes from a single source. In holoplexity theory, that source is consciousness. Velmans does not make this assertion; rather he refers to the single source as the universe. Velmans identifies the perceptual projection problem and admits he does not know how it works.

Sentience

Sentience is a term used here to refer to *self-referential* awareness specific to humans. It is hypothesized that human beings are not born with sentience. Rather, they achieve it as a developmental milestone, typically in infancy or early childhood. In this work, sentience is proposed to be a key concept of the neurocognitive concept of self (COS) as well as the embodied, self-referential "I" which is presumed to be encoded into all incoming sensory streams.

Storyline

The *storyline* is a technique that refers to the strategy of assisting the integration, creation, and formulation of the presentation of research findings in a story format narrative with a plot, beginning, middle, and end. Whether or not expressed as such, the process of grounded theory research is, in fact, a story (Birks & Mills, 2015). In this work, it is the *story* of how the researcher himself became interested in the hard problem of consciousness, how the researcher researched the problem from existing literature, what was added and changed from existing concepts, and what theory was generated from the research. The plot could be expressed in terms of the research goal and the research hypothesis.

Substantive Codes

Substantive codes, according to Birks and Mills (2015), are taken from the descriptive language of the data and typically are in the form of gerunds or *in vivo* codes. "Explanatory gap" by Levine, "perceptual projection" by Velmans, and "extra ingredient" by Chalmers would be examples of substantive codes. In this work, substantive codes were useful in identifying the parameters of the hard problem of consciousness within this study. They were also instrumental in delineating the easy problems of consciousness from the hard problem of consciousness and distinguishing consciousness itself from human consciousness.

Temporary Sentience Acquisition System

The temporary sentience acquisition system, or TSAS, is a term coined by the author to describe a set of brain mechanisms that are temporary in early infant human development that appear to play a crucial role in the formation of the self-referential, neurocognitive concept of self (COS). In this work, such a presumed system is necessary for a human infant to realize that he/she exists, therefore developing a neurocognitive concept of self (COS).

Theoretical Integration

Theoretical integration, according to Birks and Mills (2015), refers to the combining of abstract concepts into a novel grounded theory. In this work, many of the theoretical concepts are not created by the author but existed within the literature (the data). As such, many times only a theoretical concept (and not the entire theory) is used as a part of the resulting theory. Examples of theoretical integration are the concepts of "panpsychism" and "emergence." These concepts were not created nor discovered by the author but remain integral concepts in the resultant grounded theory.

Theoretical Saturation

Theoretical saturation, according to Birks and Mills (2015), refers to the occurrence of continuing research only adding to existing codes within a particular category, as opposed to identifying new codes. In this work, "dual-aspect" as a concept appeared under several different names, however once re-coded as "dual-aspect" it was realized that dual-aspect as a category was *saturated* among the twenty-three theories of consciousness.

Theory

Theory is a term used here to denote a set of interrelated hypotheses used to provide a conceptual model to provide a greater intellectual understanding of a phenomenon. In this work, "theory" does *not* mean that it is a substantiated account of human consciousness or consciousness itself. Rather, "theory" in this study refers to the *coherence* of the interrelated hypotheses contained within it, relative to the hard problem of consciousness.

Unfolding

Unfolding is a technical term used by the author to conceptualize something as expanding in complexity from a prior simpler version of itself. In this work, as the clearest example, the author refers back to the "unfolding" of 3-D visual information from two overlapping streams of 2-D visual information. A second example is 3-D information being "unfolded" from 2-D tactile information in the Bach-y-Rita and Kercel (2003) study.

Organization of the Book

Chapter 1

The introduction makes a case for the significance of "the hard problem of consciousness," contextualizes the work within the field of consciousness studies and provides an introduction to the basics of a comprehensive approach to consciousness. Also in this chapter, the theoretical basis of the study is given and analyzed, in addition to the most relevant literature as-synthesized and critically analyzed. The purpose statement is succinctly made explicit, along with the research question and the underlying overall hypothesis of this study. Key terminology is given and defined as a point of reference and to introduce some readers to some of the more esoteric concepts.

Chapter 2

Literature review contextualizes the hard problem of consciousness within the literature and provides the raw data for this study. This chapter also presents a critical synthesis of the larger themes, justifies how the study addresses the problem in the literature, and outlines the conceptual framework for providing a proposed solution to the hard problem of consciousness. In addition to providing historical background and examining existing theory relevant to the research question and the associated overall hypothesis of the study.

Chapter 3

The chapter on methodology situates the study within a particular methodological tradition, grounded theory, which is appropriate to its *type* of study. This chapter also describes the research setting, the data collection and analysis methods, as well as provides a detailed description of all the aspects of the design and procedures of this study. Information about human participants in this study is provided in this chapter.

Chapter 4

The chapter on findings organizes and reports the main findings of the *research phase* of the study. Within the appropriate narrative storyline tradition, findings are reported in plain language in a story-like sequential fashion. Findings are reported and flow logically from the problem, research question, and research design. Headings are used to guide the reader through the findings according to the research question, various themes discovered, and other organizational strategies. This chapter also provides foreshadowing as to the direction of the final two chapters. It is the research findings that direct and drive the generation of the evolving theory.

Chapter 5

The chapter on analysis and synthesis provides a discussion of the findings as they relate to the research question, the literature review, and the conceptual framework. The identification of patterns and themes is aspect detailed in this chapter. There is no clear or accepted single *right way* to analyze or interpret qualitative data. Generally, this chapter offers an opportunity to reflect thoroughly on the study findings, including its possible theoretical implications.

Chapter 6

The concluding chapter is a presentation of concluding statements and recommendations. Conclusions are assertions that are based on, warranted by, and grounded in the research. The recommendations are the application of the conclusions. Limitations are identified as potential weaknesses of the substance and scope of the study. This chapter contains the written general reflections of the contribution the author feels he has made to the knowledge and practice within the study of consciousness. It is a validation for the entrance of the research into the ranks of the body of scholars in the field.

Literature Review

Within the systematic methodology of *grounded theory* literature, it remains controversial as to whether to conduct a preliminary literature review (Glaser, 2005). For this study, however, it was necessary to conduct an overview of the field to preclude the notion that this new and evolving theory was not duplicative of any existing, contemporary theory of consciousness (Hallberg, 2010). In the preliminary literature review, it was satisfactorily demonstrated to the author that this proposed theory was substantially different in several aspects from any existing, contemporary theory, indicating that it is, in fact, a new theoretical contribution to the field of study.

The Strategy of the Literature Review

The purpose of this study is to generate a novel theory from current existing theories. This means that it is *not* a function or purpose to suggest any of the book as *hard evidence* or proof of the theory. Instead, this literature review draws upon existing theory and research to further advance like-theory. Existing relevant contemporary theory was examined and information was selected and presented when that information advanced specific theoretical issues discovered during the research.

As mentioned in the introductory chapter, great care was taken to limit the scope of the study. Theoretical issues involving questions not directly involved in answering the research question of the hard problem of consciousness were purposefully excluded. This limitation tended to create a focus on the more *theoretically oriented* works because of the *conceptual depth* of this kind of theory. More *empirically oriented* works were included when they advanced the theoretical issues of clarification and definition.

Within the study of consciousness, there are many levels to consider. Human beings are intimately aware of human consciousness, which is quite possibly only one type of many thousands. Human beings are also aware that animals possess another kind, thereby creating an example of one distinction in the levels and kinds of a larger more basic consciousness of which there may be an ever-increasing number. The point is that as the levels approach the most basic level or levels, there tends *not* to be nomenclature, vocabulary, or adequate agreed-upon language by which to describe these various phenomena.

Theories of Consciousness

The Holoplexity Theory of Consciousness was generated largely from contemporary, existing theory consistent with the chosen systematic methodology of grounded theory. The literature that was selected contained theories that constituted (a) an overview of major basic theories and (b) the approaches to understanding consciousness. The theories were broadly separated into *theoretically-based* theories and *empirically-based* theories. The dichotomy between *empirical* and *theoretical* is an artificial one that was used only to help the author organize his own thinking. As the study progressed, the author was able to see that each theory had something useful to contribute. The research itself became a question of focus and that focus became specific to a level of inquiry. The truths of the many theories were often limited to a specific level of inquiry, thus their usefulness to this research was limited to that specific level.

It is important to note that the *literature itself is the data* of this study. This literature review is not meant to give an exhaustive review of the multiple disciplines involved in the study of consciousness but, instead, to give a general overview of the *most relevant* theories of consciousness concerning the research question of the hard problem of consciousness.

Theoretically Based Theories of Consciousness

Biological naturalism theory

Searle (1993, 2000, 2017) advocated for a theory of consciousness that stated it is a "biological product" created by brain mechanisms or neural correlates without being reduced to them. Thus, consciousness is considered an *emergent* phenomenon. Consciousness is thought to be the product of what Searle calls the *unified field of consciousness* which is correlated closely with brain mechanisms but falls short of giving a definitive causal explanation of *exactly how* consciousness arises from the underlying neural correlates (Revonsuo, 2010). Searle merely creates a *category* of consciousness and thus states it cannot be reduced further (to its neurological substrates) because it is its own *category* (Searle, 2017). This tautological assertion does nothing to explain human consciousness or consciousness itself.

Stating that something itself comes from another thing, but is not reducible to that second thing, is the definition of "brute emergence" (Strawson, 2006, p. 18). Brute emergence as a concept is bothersome as it is almost indistinguishable from *a miracle*.

Searle's theory of biological naturalism also begs the question of *epiphenomenalism*, the idea that consciousness exists as a phenomenal experience only because it is thought to influence *nothing* and is *superfluous*. To the author, being "a product" of something else means that it has no part in the creation of itself. However, the theory of biological naturalism provides examples of the theoretical issues of *emergence* and *epiphenomenalism*.

Dual-content theory

Carruthers (2017) wrote a theory in 2000 and then refined it in 2005. The theory was initially written as a kind of higher-order thought (HOT) theory, but it was later revised significantly and thus differentiated enough such that it was deemed to have a unique place among this category of theories. The key significant difference is that percepts are believed to have both *first-order properties* and *higher-order contents*. As such, the name was changed to a more accurately descriptive name. It was changed from the *dispositionalist higher-order thought theory* to *dual-content theory* (Carruthers, 2017).

This theory, as refined, is *highly compatible* with the theory proposed here on several important points. First, the key theoretical issue seen in this theory is that precepts were oversimplified into a single category, but are now believed to be more dynamic than previously thought by Carruthers. This increase in dynamics tends to suggest the presence of multiple aspects of precepts. Such greater dynamics may further suggest inherent dimensions by which to facilitate the multiple simultaneous roles. Without expressly stating it, Carruthers derives a kind of dual-aspect panpsychism in the development of his theory. Carruthers himself questions, "Can the generation of such contents be explained adequately and in a naturalistically acceptable manner?" (Carruthers, 2017, p. 195).

The second key theoretical issue found in Carruthers' dual-content theory is his postulation of a "mind-reading or theory-of-mind faculty" (Carruthers, 2017, p. 294) that can effectively access concepts of experience and perceptual input both. These particular concepts are important theoretical distinctions of this theory versus other theories.

Further, Carruthers (2017) indicated that the "mind-reading or theory-of-mind" (p. 294) mechanism or "consumer system" (p. 295) can transform first-order perceptual contents. This is important because Carruthers believed that this mechanism helps a human "acquire three-dimensional distal intentional contents, representing the positions and movements of objects in space" (p. 295). Carruthers indicates 3-D information ultimately coming from tactile inputs (2-D information) from his reference to the Bach-y-Rita and Kercel (2003) study.

Emergentism theory

Vision (2017) describes a view of consciousness as a separate but irreducible property of its neural correlates. Vision argues that the history of scientific thought supports this contention. Vision further asserts that because he specifically states consciousness is not identical to its underlying correlates, his theory is not relegated to the *error of identification* (Chalmers, 1995, 2017). Essentially, Vision creates a new scientific category of *emergent* in which the underlying physical phenomena *do not have to* fully explain the emergent phenomena. Rather, it is enough to simply state that the phenomenon appears to emerge from whatever underlying physical matter. Vision (2017) states, "If we have come this far, it seems more natural just to acknowledge that novelties can arise from certain complexly structured entities" (p. 346).

The issue of emergence is key here. "Emergence" was seen as substantially similar to the claim previously made by Searle (2000, 2005, 2017) in the theory of biological naturalism, except here it is made explicit. In the opinion of this researcher, the same criticism of Searle's arguments also applies here. Brute emergence amounts to a kind of *miracle*, which is again a violation of natural law. As Vision (2017) remarks, "*[J]ust ... acknowledge ... novelties*"—because—"*complexly structured*" (p. 346), but this is not a viable argument.

Higher-order awareness theories

Higher-order awareness (HOA) theories hypothesize an *oversight* component of consciousness (Blackmore, 2004; Carruthers, 2000, 2017). HOA theories include higher-order thought (HOT) theories and higher-order perception (HOP) theories. Both subtypes (HOT and HOP) can be thought of as representational theories, in that they begin with the belief that external phenomena have representations within the mind (Dretske, 2012). This is an important distinction as many theorists believe external phenomena have no representations in the mind (primarily).

HOAs make a distinction between first-ordered thoughts or perceptions and higher-order thoughts or perceptions. First-order thoughts are the mind's representation of something. The higher-ordered perception would be that first-order thought being apprehended by a second thought or perception; akin to *metacognition* (Rosenthal, 2012). As one can see, the distinction between *thought* and *perception* in this understanding of HOA is minimal and possibly semantic only. While both these theories add something to the understanding of consciousness; each explains little in addressing the *hard problem of consciousness*, or the *explanatory gap* of phenomenality.

The distinction between first-ordered thoughts versus higher-ordered thoughts is important, but not for the reasons given within the original theory. For this author, this difference among thought structure(s) may be suggestive of where or how 3-D information may *unfold* and *become dynamic* with the inclusion of continuous incoming information. Further, the concept that one *thought* may oversee another *thought* is integral later regarding the larger *concept of self* or COS.

Modern representationalism theory

Seager and Bourget (2017) delineated this theory, designed to be compatible with naturalistic theories of mind, in contrast to classical representationalism. According to Seager and Bourget (2017):

> MR (modern representationalism) provides a powerful account of the mind which incorporates conscious experience in a way that seems intuitively satisfying, avoids difficulties associated with CR (classical representationalism), opens the door for a variety of naturalistic theories of mind, and integrates introspection without making the implausible requirement that all conscious beings have the conceptual equipment necessary to think about mental states as such. (p. 284)

This theory of consciousness represents a paradigm shift in thinking about consciousness. This theory gives weight to the idea that human perception is not necessarily a 1:1 ratio with reality and therefore opens the door for the possibility of reality being far more dynamic, subtle, and mysterious than previously imagined. This theory is still developing, and this development represents more of a way of thinking about human consciousness (as procedural) rather than a complete theory of consciousness itself (as substantive).

The MR theory in this developing phase is compatible with the proposed theory in that it *allows for* multiple dynamic processes while allowing humans potentially apprehend aspects of those processes. Importantly, Seager and Bourget (2017) further indicate *inherent reflexivity* by posing the following question: "What exactly is involved in introspection if not some kind of reflexivity intrinsic to consciousness?" (p. 284).

Multiple drafts theory

Dennett (1991) delineates his theory of consciousness in the book *Consciousness Explained.* According to Dennett, Cartesian dualism is a myth. Instead, Dennett proposes that all mental functions of the brain are accomplished in parallel, simultaneous processes that are under constant revision, hence the term multiple drafts. Dennett's theory details a kind of automaticity that can be recalled by utilizing a separate mental function; upon completion, the system goes back to a kind of serial independent processing (Revonsuo, 2010). This theory is a functionalist theory in which human consciousness is reduced to a byproduct of these multiple drafts resulting in a kind of perception in the brain as an epiphenomenon.

Naturalistic dualism theory

Chalmers (1995, 2017b) wrote a theory of consciousness entitled *Naturalistic Dualism.* Chalmers theorized the existence of *proto-consciousness,* which he defined as *instances of consciousness that are so fundamental* that we may not even recognize them as consciousness. Chalmers theorizes that these instances of consciousness are amplified in the brain into the consciousness that we recognize today as human consciousness (Blackmore, 2014; Chalmers, 2017b). Chalmers (2017a) gives an overview of other theories of consciousness and points out the need for a type of "extra ingredient" (p. 39).

The above framework of consciousness theorizing is the most compatible with the proposed theory. It is Chalmers's general framework (2017a) that served as the theoretical framework for this study. Chalmers" work is considered seminal in the field and integral to the organizational structure of this work. It is Chalmers' (1996) question that was reinterpreted by the author and is ultimately the research question here—*how does information become experience?*

Neurophenomenology theory

Varela (1995) proposed what amounts to a theory of consciousness, known as *neurophenomenology*. Neurophenomenology theory also doubles as a useful methodological remedy for the difficulties of distinguishing consciousness in the reductionistic paradigm of western science. Neurophenomenology proposed that the nature of consciousness was such that it could not be reduced to anything more fundamental. The substantive theory itself is most like the sensorimotor theory of consciousness by O'Regan and Noe (2001) in that it is the complex interaction between body and environment that produces our phenomenological experience of consciousness. It is not the body itself, but the "body as phenomenally experienced" in its interactions with the environment.

Like Bourget and Seager's modern representationalism, this work represents a paradigm that seems to be shifting within the search for a comprehensive account of consciousness. Abandoned are the short-sighted, rigid ways of thinking about consciousness. Interestingly, the lines between the substantive aspects of theories of consciousness and the necessarily related procedural ways of looking at them are blurring. This suggests to the researcher that the ultimate reality that we are pursuing has aspects of both *substance* and *process* that co-occur.

Physicalist panpsychism theory

Strawson (2017) provided an eloquent argument regarding the nature of consciousness as the stuff of which all other substance is comprised, including consciousness as experienced by humans. This theoretical perspective is included as a contemporary theory of consciousness in *The Blackwell Companion to Consciousness (2nd ed.)* (2017); however, no specific mention of how it arises as human consciousness is given.

Reflexive monism theory

Velmans' (1990, 2008, 2017) theory of *Reflexive Monism* proposed a systematic paradigm shift in thinking about consciousness as it relates to subjectivism and science. This theory is an attempt to reconcile the schism between "subjectivism" and "objectivism," or the split between first- and third-person perspectives (Velmans, 2017a, 2017b). It offers no new evidence but proposes a paradigm shift in perspective that can eliminate the scientific bias toward explicit objective observations, essentially by stating there exists no real dichotomy because all observations are subjective (as all from a *subjective* first-person perspective initially).

For Velmans (1990, 2008, 2017a, 2017b), this age-old dichotomy is the result of an epistemological misinterpretation of the ontology of *subjectivity* in relation to *objectivity*. However, the reflexive monism theory lends conceptual support to the developing theory. Velmans (2008) states:

> While such studies all contribute to our understanding of space perception, including perceptual projection viewed as a psychological effect, they do not explain how proximal neural causes within the brain support visually experienced events that seem to be outside the brain. For this, we require an added explanatory model—and no adequate explanatory model currently exists. (p. 20)

This proposed theory amounts to an explanatory model sufficient to address this explicitly stated need. The researcher believes that this theory joins the dual-content theory in suggesting phenomena not currently hypothesized to exist but that are explicitly hypothesized within this proposed theory. The explicit phenomena are that consciousness itself constitutes a dimension and that information unfolds within that dimension—the consequence of which is interpreted as the passage of time.

Sensorimotor theory

O'Regan and Noe (2001) deny the phenomenality of consciousness and replace it with the interaction of one's environment and internal body maps. O'Regan and Noe argue that an internal re-creation of the external is not necessary as the external is its own representation. Consciousness is defined as *an embodied interaction with the world.* As such, consciousness is not derived from brain activity directly.

This theory is most similar to the work of Damasio and a handful of other theorists, who view the body (any part, including the eye) and environmental interaction as a kind of cognition (i.e., the Santiago theory). It is the considered opinion of the researcher that this thinking is necessarily correct, but it was too circumscribed to address the larger question of the hard problem of consciousness. The researcher believes that this framework is partially concurrent with the hard problem of consciousness. This framework was likely a precursor to the development of the frontal cortex specializing in isolating explicit thinking. Today, it is part and parcel of an existing system of juxtaposing thoughts and thought-like elements (i.e., emotion) as they occur within the human brain—therefore partially applicable to the hard problem of consciousness.

Virtual reality theory

Metzinger (2009), Lehar (2003), and Klemm (2014) wrote theories consistent with a virtual reality theory of reality and consciousness. In virtual reality theory, consciousness exists within the confines of the human brain; consciousness and virtual realities are mostly one and the same; all our experienced *realities* are being experienced within that *virtual reality* (Blackmore, 2004). Metzinger (2009) makes an analogy of a pilot being born into a flight simulator in which all humans are the *pilot,* and the *flight simulator* is everything else we believe is the objective reality.

This is an interesting cluster of theories that may eventually turn out to be correct. However, to the researcher, these theories tend to answer questions of phenomenology. These theories are silent as to the origins of where the brain gets its information and the nature of that information, and this is the nature of what the hard problem seeks. These theories tend to *begin* where any potential answer to the hard problem of consciousness would leave off.

Empirically Based Theories of Consciousness

Dynamic core theory

Edelman and Tononi (2000) delineated a theory of consciousness in *A Universe of Consciousness: How Matter Becomes Imagination.* In their theoretical conception, consciousness is created by a *dynamic core* made up of an integrated set of neural components that interact continuously with each other. The specific neural components may change, but it is the continuity and integration that keeps the *core* intact through its numerous recurrent loops. It is differentiated from global workspace theories in that it is the *amount* of input, rather than its widespread distribution, that causes consciousness.

This theory is the first iteration of an eventual second theory by Tononi (2004), the *Information Integration Theory.* Tononi's evolution of theories mimics the larger evolution of the search for an understanding of consciousness within science and philosophy. Both theories begin by examining *human consciousness* as more or less synonymous with *consciousness itself,* then move to examine a more basic kind of consciousness as *consciousness itself.* Tononi, a physician, limits himself in both theories to understanding human consciousness as it exists in the human brain. However, in the second theory, Tononi realizes that human consciousness cannot be merely brain function and consequently expands his and Edelman's theory to include *information* as understood within information theory. Pursuing consciousness outside the confines of the human brain is a similar path that this researcher took in pursuing an answer to the pressing question of how *information becomes experience* (as reformulated by Chalmers, 2017b).

Global workspace theories

Baars' (2005) article *Global workspace theory of consciousness: toward a cognitive neuroscience of human experience* contends that the human cognitive system operates against a global workspace that is analogous to a stage in the theater of the mind (Baars, 2005). The theater has inputs from the senses and all other areas of the brain. The inputs compete among themselves for primacy. Once primacy is achieved, that input has attained consciousness (not unlike the multiple drafts theory). Consciousness then means that a specific input becomes available to the rest of the brain. It is unclear whether this *workspace* is synonymous with *working memory*. It is suggested that this *globalization* of the contents of the *workspace* is what constitutes consciousness for Baars.

In Dehaene's (2014) book *Consciousness and the brain: deciphering how the brain codes our thoughts,* he delineates *Global Neuronal Workspace Theory* (GNW) which superficially appears to be an elaboration upon *Global Workspace Theory* (GWT); instead, it focuses specifically on the electromagnetic mechanisms involved.

These theories are important because they inaugurate the concept of the mind as being a dynamic process rather than a static thing. The theorists also introduce the concept that ideas and mind are manifested as/in and transmitted by electricity within the human brain. This is both a crucial development and perhaps indicative of the true nature of consciousness.

Implicate order theory

Bohm (1980) wrote a comprehensive theory of matter and its relationship to the mind. Educated as a physicist, Bohm begins his theory at the level of quantum physics. Bohm is not categorized with the other quantum theorists because his theory focuses on the continuum of consciousness from consciousness itself through human consciousness, whereas the quantum theorists tended to focus on mental causation within the brain. Bohm hypothesized the existence of *holomovement* in which movement itself is fundamental and everything else is derivative. Movement is thought to give rise to fields, and fields constitute matter.

Once on the classical level, matter behaves the way that classical physics has established. An electron is thought to have two aspects: a field aspect, and a particle aspect. The field aspect contains *active information* which guides the particle. This is a two-way relationship; the notion of "back-action" (Sarfatti, 1997) states that the particle may also influence its own field. If the "field" is conceived of as "mental" and the "particle" as "physical", then this would be a viable solution to the mind/body problem and tend to explain mental causation.

Information integration theory

Tononi (2004) wrote a new theory that expanded upon a previous theory as delineated in the book *A Universe of Consciousness: How Matter Becomes Imagination* (Edelman & Tononi, 2000). In it, the *dynamic core* was responsible for generating consciousness. In this current theory, more detail is given as to how exactly that is achieved on a micro level. It is proposed that information contains *particles of consciousness*. The dynamic core distributes and integrates this information in such a manner as to give rise to consciousness as we know it (Revonsuo, 2010; Tononi, 2017a, 2017b).

The development of this secondary theory by Tononi seemed to reflect the fact that consciousness was unlikely to be a wholly brain-generated phenomenon. This theory bridges a conceptual gap between the *information/electricity focus* within consciousness studies and how that *information/electricity* may be made into human consciousness via the dynamic core.

Intermediate-level theory of consciousness

Prinz (2017) updated and reiterated a theory of consciousness first espoused by Ray Jackendoff in 1987. Prinz admits that Jackendoff himself did not proffer this theory as a fully-fledged theory of consciousness, but Prinz adds emphasis to the single missing part: *attention*. The updated theory was similar to Tononi's Information Integration Theory (and was somewhat arguably duplicative). However, it is useful in strengthening the notion that consciousness itself seems to be a process of combining specific energies.

This theory is important because it buttresses the growing opinion that the mind has an integral relationship with electricity in its quasi-computer and information processing capabilities. However, Tononi's *Information Integration Theory* offers a more comprehensive model of consciousness. The missing piece offered by Prinz was delineated by Tononi and Edelman's dynamic core but stated somewhat differently by calling it *integration* as opposed to *attention*. The researcher hypothesizes that *integration* is the larger term, whereas *attention* is the phenomenal *result* of integration and subsequent interaction with the dynamic core.

Microconsciousness theory

Zeki (1999) proposes that overall consciousness consists of many *microconsciousnesses* combined. This is distinct from *panpsychism* because there is no claim that these microconsciousnesses are found outside the brain, nor independent of brain mechanisms. Zeki denies the need for a *Cartesian theater* for these microconsciousnesses to become conscious. It is upon the completion of *neural processing* that neural activity becomes *rendered explicit* or conscious. This neural activity is rendered explicit and distributed within the brain, not throughout space and time.

This was another interesting theory that may ultimately turn out to be conceptually accurate but is irrelevant to the hard problem of consciousness. However, it should be noted that this conjecture indirectly lends support to the notion of panpsychism, as well as the hypothesis that a *dynamic core* or other *circular device* is necessary for consciousness itself to apprehend itself.

Neurobiological theory

Crick & Koch (1990; 1994) wrote a framework theorizing that synchronized phase-locked firing at 40-hertz oscillation may be the neural correlate of the content of consciousness. Later, they recanted that synchronized firing was sufficient to account for a complete and total explanation of consciousness. Crick and Koch's framework is similar to Baar's theory of GWT and Dehaene's GNW theory.

This theory is important as it represents specific progress toward the broader notion that consciousness itself may be manifest as, and not just transported by, electricity. Although this notion is still unclear, the progression of the literature seems to be moving in that direction.

Quantum consciousness theories

Atmanspacher (2017) gave an overview of the field of quantum approaches to consciousness. It concluded: "The overall conclusion is that the application of quantum field theory describes how classical behavior emerges at the level of brain activity considered. The relevant brain states themselves are viewed as classical states" (p. 303). This is added here because it is a relevant *theory* about the non-applicability of quantum physics at the level of classical physics with brain states being defined as classical states.

In the opinion of the author, consciousness itself does exist at the quantum level of analysis. Therefore, quantum theories have a place in this analysis, but as demonstrated time and again, quantum effects do not reach the level of classical physics. The researcher believes that this is the case with consciousness itself, too; except that an aspect of consciousness seems to have something that *does survive* the quantum/classical physics transition. What survives that transition? What is the mechanism that creates the spatial *from* the non-spatial? The researcher hypothesized that it is the transition from possibility/probability into the realm of reality. The evidence seems to be seen in the *double-slit experiment* thereby suggesting to the researcher that an aspect of consciousness itself survives the quantum/classical dichotomy.

Eccles (1994) wrote a book detailing a quantum-based theory of consciousness that seems to work in its non-quantum aspects. Eccles proposes an interaction between psychons and dendrons to overcome the problem of epiphenomenalism. This part of the theory seems to hold promise, but it is unclear on exactly how quantum mechanisms would influence macro neurons on a scale large enough to be significant. With interpretation, Eccles' theory can be seen as advocating for a double aspect, which is seen in the literature and the most likely cause.

Hameroff and Penrose (1996) wrote a consciousness theory proposing that the problems of such as the unity consciousness, binding, and non-computational aspects of consciousness are possibly explained by quantum effects occurring in the microtubules of the brain. To explain the effect, Hameroff and Penrose introduce a new physical phenomenon of *wave function self-collapse* that they term *objective reduction* (OR). Other microtubules act as *nodes* to and are thought to *orchestrate* (Orch) microtubule coherence (OR). It is proposed that *intentionality* may inhere in the process of orchestration; orchestration itself is a kind of *unity* through *binding* within the orchestration process.

McGinn (1995) wrote a work entitled *Consciousness and space*. In the article, it is postulated that consciousness predates matter in the big bang and that consciousness has a hidden dimension or principle. The idea that consciousness has a hidden dimension or principle is significant. This idea tends to echo Chalmers' idea that there is a missing "extra ingredient" among the many theories of consciousness. This idea is integral to this proposed theory.

Recurrent processing theory

Lamme's (2006) theory on consciousness itself, distinguished from other phenomena such as attention, language, subjectivity, qualia, reportability, and others, identifies consciousness as synonymous with the slower recurrent processing occurring one hundred to three hundred milliseconds from stimulus onset. This distinction has the advantage of moving consciousness studies fully into the domain of neuroscience by eliminating the subjective aspect of consciousness. This theory is very similar and shares many features with Tononi's *Information Integration Theory* and Llinas's *Binding Theory* but does not specifically include the (deeper) thalamocortical system.

This theory is useful because it represents a possible attempt to isolate *consciousness itself* from *human consciousness*, although that is somewhat unclear. Much of what Lamme distinguished from *consciousness itself* is similar to the phenomena that Chalmers declared constitutive of the easy problems of consciousness (leaving only the hard problem). Some of the easy problems of consciousness are relevant to the hard problem of consciousness, whereas others are mere brain function and are not relevant to this study.

Santiago theory

The Santiago theory of cognition, written by Maturana and Varela (1972), is a holistic, systemic theory of life. The central concept of the Santiago theory of cognition is *autopoiesis*—the activity of self-generation and self-perpetuation in living systems. The Santiago theory of cognition is a radical expansion of the term "cognition" to apply to all forms of life and of course to the concept of mind.

Importantly, the Santiago theory of cognition does *not* hold that "consciousness itself" is a causal factor in cognition. As a theory regarding life processes, the Santiago theory holds that "human consciousness" emerges as a product of the complex, non-linear dynamics of neural activity. The Santiago theory has several overlapping similarities to Damasio's somatic marker theory as well as Tononi's information integration theory.

Somatic marker theory

Damasio (1996, 1999) wrote a theory of consciousness that proposes emotions play an integral part in consciousness. Damasio's theory is not unlike higher-order awareness (HOA) theories, with the exception that emotion is seen as a *dispositional* mental construct and therefore subject to secondary apprehension by a *self*. In Damasio's theory, the secondary thought or perception would be by the *self*. Damasio makes a distinction between *core consciousness* and an *extended consciousness* in which *core consciousness* is a basic here-and-now consciousness that human beings share with animals, and extended consciousness is a dynamic, reflexive phenomenon when coupled with a *self*.

Damasio's work suggests phylogenetically how cognitive consciousness may have developed somatically via the juxtaposition of bodily information combined with other brain-based information. This explanation seems plausible to the researcher because when different sources of information are juxtaposed in space and then combined, it opens up the possibility of a more dynamic way of thinking, such as going from 2-D to 3-D, to modern-day 4-D. The specialization of lateral brain compartments tends to do this, along with the specialization of the three levels of the brain's phylogenic development. To the researcher, such development would allow for incoming consciousness stimuli to *unfold*.

Thalamocortical binding theory

Llinas (2002) delineated a theory of consciousness known as *the thalamocortical binding theory* in a book entitled *I of the Vortex.* The theory itself is substantially similar to the dynamic core theory and the information integration theory as proposed by Edelman and Tononi (2000), and Tononi (2004). However, significant differences in Llinas's theory include the primacy of the role of the reticular nucleus of the thalamus and the bi-directionality of thalamocortical loops. It is the thalamocortical bi-directional loop that provides the phenomenally unified perceptual world humans experience.

This theory constitutes another possible iteration of how a neurocognitive *self* can relate to the information that comprises its environment. Theory does not prove theory, but it does tend to give support to certain ideas, such as *loop* as integral in the development of *self*. As any theory approaches conceptual accuracy, the number of iterations of its components will be increasingly reflected in other theoretical models. The researcher feels as if this is an example of that phenomenon.

Conceptual framework

A conceptual framework draws upon theory, research, and evidence and then examines the relationships between the various constructs and ideas contained in the representative theories. These are the theoretical and methodological bases of development for this study and the subsequent analysis of its findings. This qualitative study was undertaken by rigorously applying the tenets of the systematic methodology of grounded theory. Grounded theory as a design is a systematic, qualitative procedure used to generate new theory—which in turn explains a process, an action, or an interaction about a substantive topic at a broad conceptual level. Grounded theory refers to an inductive, general method used to build new theory.

The novel theory generated by this approach was recursively tied back to additional existing data and is conceptually consistent with specific aspects of said data. The purpose of this study was not only to generate new theory but also to transparently show how the newly created theory relates conceptually to existing theory—and to show how some specific aspects were intellectually surmised from specific existing theory.

Within the study at hand, a qualitative constant comparative analysis *searches* for the existing building blocks of the study of consciousness to lay the foundation of the building of this newly proposed theory. Utilizing the methods of synthesis and abduction, an *original*, empirically compatible, and nonreductive theory of consciousness was generated. It was hypothesized to be sufficient to answer the hard problem of consciousness.

The researcher examined and reviewed the existing data and then used that data to *ground* and *develop* the newly proposed theory. As such, this proposed theory was *grounded*, and therefore, conceptually supported at nearly all levels of development. The proposed theory also provides answers to several sub-problems associated with the *hard problem of consciousness* as discovered in the literature during researching this issue.

Summary

Consciousness does not have a widely agreed-upon definition or a comprehensive unifying theory. *Human consciousness itself* has not been distinguished from *consciousness itself*. There is a general consensus that human consciousness, in some form, exists. Whether human consciousness exists as a superfluous phenomenon or as a byproduct of neuronal function is another question that arises here.

Some other relevant questions that arise include: what is the metaphysical nature of *human consciousness*? Does the nature of *human consciousness* imply the existence of *consciousness itself* as an independent entity? How and why does *human consciousness* appear to be generated within the human brain? And how does this cause mere *information* to result in dynamic *experience*? These are huge questions. However, as the reader will see—this review of the literature also contains a great many suggestions, hints, and even "evidence" toward the resolutions of these questions.

For instance, *panpsychism* seems to be emerging as a viable conceptual solution to aspects of the questions of *consciousness itself*, as seen directly in Strawson's physicalist panpsychism theory, Chalmers' naturalistic dualism theory, Velmans' reflexive monism theory, Carruthers' dual-content theory, Bohm's implicate order theory, and Maturana and Varela's Santiago theory of cognition. The answers are also *indirectly* seen in Zeki's microconsciousness theory as well as the work of the quantum theorists (Hameroff and Penrose, Eccles, McGinn, Atmanspacher, and Bohm as well as the HOA theorists, Rosenthal, and others.

Secondly, new ways of conceptualizing *consciousness as a phenomenon* (read: across both *consciousness itself* and *human consciousness*) are emerging, which is seen by the researcher as a step away from the intellectual dogmatism that led to the current state of mechanistic and reductionistic thinking about consciousness as a phenomenon, and a step toward more integrated and holistic thinking about all the information generated about consciousness. This new integrated thinking is most readily seen in the works of Varela (neurophenomenology theory) as well as Seager and Bourget (modern representationalism theory) and again in that of Velmans, Chalmers, Bohm, Maturana, and Varela. Newly integrated thinking can be seen indirectly in the works of virtual reality theorists, quantum theorists, and global workspace theorists. The term *integrated thinking* is defined by the researcher as the kind of thinking that necessarily considers "brain physiology" as equally important to "conscious experience" and treats them as two interdependent domains.

Finally, there is a growing number of theories (i.e., global workspace theories) that hypothesize electricity as related, in some manner, to the phenomenon of consciousness; all the empirically-based theories of consciousness recognize the role of electricity or energy. As the term *empirical* connotes, these theories are presumed to be more *scientifically oriented*, or as anointed by a third-person legitimization. This recognition of electricity may be indicative that electricity is the mechanism by which human beings transmit and organize consciousness within their bodies. Another possibility is that this is how an *unembodied potential* influences physical reality from beyond some unseen boundary. Perhaps that boundary, like the boundary of classical physics, is demarcated by the speed of light. Perhaps thinking this way is in itself mechanistic thinking, as the notion of "time" is inherent within "speed"?

Conclusion

It appears to the researcher that a *necessary* and sufficient body of knowledge *does exist* to create an original, empirically compatible, nonreductive theory of consciousness with the addition of a handful of theoretical mechanisms as well as a new theoretical perspective. Concepts that are theoretically consistent may be adopted from each theory to create foundational knowledge upon which to predicate a new theory of consciousness from a new perspective. *All that is left is to do it.*

Methodology

The purpose of this chapter is to provide an introduction and overview of the systematic research methodology of this qualitative study. Grounded Theory (GT) is the research methodology in which new theory is advanced from existing theory. GT is the appropriate methodology to attempt to provide a plausible theoretical answer to the hard problem of consciousness. This approach provides for a greater understanding of existing consciousness theories, the issues of epistemology and ontology in the literature, and a deeper understanding of the hard problem of consciousness. The efficacy of grounded theory as well as the constructivist approach is discussed in this chapter. The research strategy itself, including methodology, procedures, analysis method, and quality processes are also examined within this chapter.

After the listing and the examination of each research component and/or strategy, examples from the study itself will be examined to illustrate the more abstract processes to illuminate the path of development of each component of this theory. All of this is done to create transparency for the entire process of the creation of this newly developed theory—especially of its transformations and its novel elements which are introduced here.

Research Question

Does sufficient data exist in the literature upon which to predicate and generate an original, empirically compatible, nonreductive theory of consciousness sufficient to answer the hard problem of consciousness? The research question is revisited here as it is useful to keep in mind the specific purpose and goal of this research while also contemplating the components of the systematic research methodology. Additionally, the highly abstract nature of the subject matter itself and the rather confusing, academic discipline-specific terms tend to obfuscate the meaning of the literature itself.

Methodology Selected

Grounded theory is the methodology of choice for this *type* of study because the outcome desired is a *new* theory generated from *existing* theory. Grounded theory is a *theory discovery methodology* (Martin & Turner, 1986). Of the many qualitative methodologies that exist today, grounded theory was the appropriate choice of methodology for this kind of qualitative research when the goal was the generation or creation of new theory.

Grounded Theory Methodology

This qualitative study was undertaken by rigorously applying the tenets of the systematic methodology of grounded theory. Grounded theory as a design is a systematic, qualitative procedure used to generate new theory, which in turn explains a process, an action, or an interaction about a substantive topic at a broad conceptual level (Creswell, 2008). Grounded theory refers to an inductive, general method used to build new theory.

The new theory created by this approach was recursively tied back to additional existing data, such that the resulting theory was consistent with specific aspects of the existing data. The purpose of this study was not only to generate a new theory but also to show clearly how the newly created, novel theory relates conceptually to existing theory. Additionally, the study includes open and detailed explanations of how some specific aspects were surmised from specific existing theory (*transparency*).

This study utilized a qualitative constant comparative analysis *search* for the existing building blocks of what was known about consciousness to lay the foundation for the building of newly proposed theory. Utilizing the grounded theory approach, specifically the methods of synthesis and abduction, a new theory was generated proposed as an *original*, empirically compatible, nonreductive theory of consciousness. This theory was also believed to be sufficient to address the hard problem of consciousness.

The existing data both grounds *and* develops the proposed theory. This proposed theory was *grounded,* thus conceptually supported, at nearly all levels of development. The proposed theory tends to provide answers to several sub-problems posed in the literature. This theory is created and offered as an answer to *the hard problem of consciousness.*

Essential grounded theory methods

The *data* for the present study was methodologically determined to be the most relevant *existing literature* on consciousness. Specifically, it began with the various *major* theories found in the existing literature at the time of this study. This broad inclusion was specifically consistent with the grounded theory data analytic notions that *all is data,* and that *everything is a concept* (Glaser, 1978). The book *The Blackwell Companion to Consciousness* (2nd ed.) by Schneider and Velmans (2017) gave a "comprehensive overview" of the consciousness literature and thus was integral in establishing the literature parameters. This was further informed by three consciousness textbooks: *Consciousness: The Science of Subjectivity* by Revonsuo (2010); *Consciousness: an Introduction* by Blackmore (2004); and *Exploring Consciousness* by Carter (2002). These four texts provided a comprehensive foundation for this study.

The text *Grounded Theory: A Practical Guide (*2nd edition*)* by Birks and Mills (2015) formed the systematic methodological basis for this study by outlining the basic essential tenets of grounded theory methodology. Birks and Mills explained in detail each procedure, such as coding, generating memos, analyzing data (as it is generated to create new theory), selecting core categories from coding, and the generation of new theory. These processes of grounded theory methodology allowed the data to be viewed as appropriately coded, conceptual abstractions as related to the overall hard problem(s) of consciousness. This process allowed for the recombination of the (appropriately coded) conceptual abstractions in such a way as to suggest a foundation for a newly created coherent account. This newly created coherent account was deemed to be conceptually adequate as to constitute a plausible answer to the hard problem of consciousness.

Initial coding and categorization of data

This is the first step of data analysis; it is a way of identifying significant concepts in the data and then *labeling* them (Birks & Mills, 2015). *In vivo* codes are typically verbatim quotes from participants, and are themselves sometimes used as labels. A *category* is a group of related codes (Halloway, 2008). Categories are said to be *saturated* when additional data analysis returns codes that only appropriately fit into *existing* categories. Such categories should be sufficiently defined in terms of their properties and limits.

An example of this first step is seen in the initial dichotomy of theories. This initial division separated approaches to thinking about consciousness into *empirically based* and *theoretically based* approaches. Such a separation is significant because of the underlying assumptions that are present in each approach. Empiricism imposed very significant restrictions upon what was able to be considered in the quest for understanding consciousness. One of those significant restrictions was the *third-party observation* limitation. *Theoretically based*, which could easily have been also named *philosophically based*, was under no such restriction. Therefore, it had a greater degree of freedom to explore the nature of what was not fully understood. The term *theoretical* was chosen over the term *philosophical* because the presumed end goal of all these theories was to not only provide an adequate explanation of consciousness but also to expand the understanding of the metaphysics of reality for all purposes, including scientific. The term *theoretical* was seen as something generated by—and common to—both the disciplines of philosophy and the sciences.

Concurrent data generation or collection and analysis

Specific to Grounded Theory as a design are the processes of "concurrent data generation" or "collection and analysis." Samples are purposefully chosen from which data are collected or generated.

This data is coded before additional data is collected or generated. This process of analysis is then generally repeated. It is this specific procedural step that tends to differentiate grounded theory from other types of research designs (Glaser & Strauss, 1967).

For this work, this step is perhaps the most important single step of systematic grounded theory methodology. An example of this step is the practice of actively discriminating *significance* as one pursues data. This is where the researcher uses the term *recursive* when applying data itself to the search for additional data. Remembering that *data* consisted of existing theory and considering the conceptual implications of each theory implied where to look for further data to advance the developing theory. As a more concrete example, if the metaphysical implications of the notion of *panpsychism* were pursued, then pursuing that direction would occur as opposed to the metaphysical implications of the notion of *emergentism*. While good scholarship requires *both* implications to be thoughtfully *considered*, concurrent data generation requires only one to be actively pursued (to avoid the generation of parallel, but conflicting data).

Theoretical sampling

When it becomes apparent that additional information is required to *saturate* categories still under development, a *strategic decision* is made regarding where to find specific compatible additional information to fulfill analytical needs (Strauss and Corbin, 1998). Theoretical sampling is the mechanism used to feed the process of constant comparative analysis. A key component of theoretical sampling is *saturation* and not representativeness; the size of the sample is *not* statistically determined (Neuman, 2003).

For this study, this step represents a key distinction. Recalling the research question of whether sufficient data exists in the literature upon which to propose a *new* theory, suggests then that this new theory must possess qualities not currently found in existing theories. This is true—otherwise, there would be no need to search for, or to generate, a new theory in answer to the hard problem of consciousness. This also means that current thinking, current theorizing, is somehow missing the mark. Going back to the *missing-keys metaphor* from chapter 1, the search is now directed to more unlikely places. Because of these circumstances, the *representativeness* of something already deemed *more unlikely* will *by definition* tend not to be statistically abundant. Thus, under these circumstances and from the outside looking in, whatever theory generated will *necessarily appear* to have little theoretical conceptual support within the literature. However, in the time it took to conduct and write this study, that level of conceptual support appears to be changing. This is the *nature of* what is being sought by this study.

Constant comparative analysis

The constant comparative analysis is defined as the process of concurrent data collection and analysis being *constantly compared* regarding incident-to-incident, incident-to-codes, codes-to-codes, codes-to-categories, and categories-to-categories (Birks and Mills, 2015). This process continues in the grounded theory design until a grounded theory is fully integrated and a new theory is developed.

For this study, this procedure is an ongoing process and is referred to by the term *concurrent* within the larger step of *concurrent data generation or collection and analysis.* The step of *concurrent data generation or collection and analysis* was the single most important step because it provided flexibility in direction while building a separate identity to the theory under construction. An example of this within the study is the *constant comparative analysis* that occurred between the theses of *panpsychism* and *emergentism* again. Both theses have pros and cons associated with them in the attempt to explain various aspects of consciousness. It was through the process of *constant comparative analysis* allowed the issues to *boil down to* whether one can accept the concept of *brute emergence*. In brute emergence, a phenomenon is not required to be explained by some virtue of its constituent parts. This logic is *unacceptable* as it is indistinguishable from that which constitutes a *miracle*; therefore, the thesis of *emergentism* was rejected.

Induction

Grounded theory methods are inductive, which means that they constitute a process of theory building from the data itself. The induction of theory occurs through this process of constant comparative analysis, from specific instances to general. This concept can again be illustrated in the clear example of *panpsychism* versus *emergentism*.

Abduction

Abduction refers to reasoning that occurs within all stages of analysis, but most notably during constant comparative analysis, specifically at the level of category-to-category which tends to lead to theoretical integration. Abduction has been described as a *cerebral process*, an *intellectual act*, or a *mental leap* that brings together concepts in a way not previously associated; it is a logic of discovery (Reichertz, 2007).

For this study, the reasoning that consciousness itself is *both* a structural foundation (aka dimension) *and* the substance which occupies that *dimension* is an example of *abduction*. A related example of abductive reasoning is that the proposed *dimension* of consciousness and its interaction with itself is the causal factor of the *time* as humans perceive it.

Intermediate coding

Intermediate coding is the second major stage of data analysis. Individual categories are developed by connecting sub-categories to fully develop their range of properties and dimensions. The categories themselves are then linked together. Initial coding may be thought of as breaking down the data, whereas intermediate coding may be thought of as reorganizing the data in conceptually abstract ways.

For this study, the term *coding* is largely synonymous with *naming, describing,* or *identifying.* But more than that, it is naming, describing, or identifying a phenomenon as specific to a distinct level of analysis. Often, there is no substantive difference, except for the level of analysis. Take for example water—at one level it is a molecule of H-O-H; at another level, it may be a droplet of rain; at another, it may be a glass of water; at another, it may constitute a cloud; at perhaps its largest level it constitutes approximately 71% of the Earth's surface. The point here is that each level is significant as to the *ability to analyze* the same substance (water). Because this study examines consciousness and proposes it is the foundation of reality, *intermediate coding* represents a kind of coordination in describing and determining *where in analysis* consciousness exists as it is being described.

Identifying a core category

Intermediate coding tends to facilitate the degree of conceptual analysis within the developing grounded theory. During this time, a core category may be selected that encapsulates and tends to explain the developing grounded theory itself. *Theoretical sampling* and *selective coding* continue the development of the core category in a highly conceptual way. Full theoretical saturation of both the core category and related categories, sub-categories, and their properties is the goal at this stage.

For this study, the core category being developed was a type of *panpsychism*. The establishment of the core category allowed for a better understanding of its relationship to other aspects of other theories as well as the ontological and epistemological issues surrounding the category. A more thorough understanding of the ontological and epistemological issues allowed for the formulation of *alternative explanations* via abduction to advance the developing theory. An example of this alternative explanation was the previously mentioned notion of consciousness constituting a dimension (or structure of reality). Because if consciousness constitutes a structure of reality, then it tends to explain the phenomenon of time and its vicissitudes, as well as explain how something can occupy one bit of space in one moment, then occupy a seemingly different bit of space the next moment. The current generally accepted conception of *time* does not provide an answer to this very basic question.

Advanced coding and theoretical integration

Advanced coding, or the creation of *themes*, is integral to theoretical integration. Advanced coding procedures include the use of *the storyline technique* to both integrate and present grounded theory.

Story is defined as, "a descriptive narrative about the central phenomenon of the study" and *storyline* is defined as, "the conceptualization of the story...the core category" (Strauss & Corbin, 1990, p. 116). Theoretical codes, or themes, may be taken from existing theories to facilitate theoretical integration while adding explanatory power to the final product. This stage also makes clear the new grounded theory's position within the existing body of knowledge. The final product is an integrated and comprehensive new grounded theory with explanatory power regarding a process or a scheme associated with a phenomenon (Birks & Mills, 2015).

The previous example of *consciousness as a dimension* is relevant to this step. *Time* as a phenomenon may seem tangential to the study of consciousness—until one considers the level of analysis. At the most basic level, *everything* will be relevant, as consciousness is proposed to be *the* underlying structure of *all reality*. If so, then consciousness must be compatible with all other physical phenomena observed in nature, including time. Therefore, if consciousness is the underlying physical structure of reality, then its existence must be *integrated* with consciousness. The proposed theory integrates these two phenomena.

Quality Processes

Preservation of Meaning

This was a study within which there were sometimes no previously established names or labels for various phenomena. When such phenomena are studied, *descriptions* are heavily used. The fact that *meaning* that is contained within these descriptions is important.

Therefore, direct quotes were utilized to preserve meaning. The use of direct quotes is analogous to the use of *in vivo* codes as a quality process intended to, again, *preserve meaning* as contained in the descriptions (as the literature *is* the data). Once this meaning was *directly* conveyed to the reader, at least once—only then were interpretive efforts made upon such meanings, to arrive at a more generalized understanding of the underlying concepts. There is no clear or accepted single *right way* to analyze or interpret qualitative data. Such information then takes the form of *substantive codes* in grounded theory.

For this study, quotations were generally avoided except when doing so may interrupt a subtle distinction in meaning contained in the exact constellation of words. Perhaps the most salient example is the quote by Velmans (2008) contained within the *Reflexive Monism Theory* summary given in the literature review of this study. Velmans' words were left undisturbed because the meaning of what was captured by them illustrates an issue within *proximal causes* that is very difficult to adequately restate or interpret without some subtle change in meaning. The subtleties and fine distinctions are very much at issue in the data (literature).

Audit Trail

Within the research approach of grounded theory, storyline as a technique and strategy will be utilized to convey meaning in a relevant, contextualized fashion. The storyline was developed to the degree that it may double to serve as *an audit trail*, detailing the management of data (meaning) and resources, while demonstrating the application of procedural logic. *Transparency* at all levels of analysis was "strived for" and demonstrated clearly. *An audit trail* is defined as, "a record of decisions made in relation to the conduct of research" (Birks & Mills, 2015, p. 177). The written *memos*, *storyline* device, and the *manuscript* itself together constitute the record of decisions made concerning this research. Regarding any aspect of the proposed theory, it is possible to go back into the manuscript and utilize the storyline and corresponding memos to recreate *how and why* a decision was made within the research.

Writing memos

Memos have been described as "intellectual capital in the bank" (Clark, 2005, p. 85). Memos are notes about the process itself of executing a grounded theory design study. The theory generated is not separate from the process that was undertaken to generate it—and memo writing is the record of that connection. Memos provide a record of how *meaning* was both transferred and preserved from step to step.

Grounded theory is silent as to the physical form of *memos*; as such the digital notes were written by the researcher to the researcher; sent from one email service (*Gmail*) to another email service (*Yahoo*) preserving copies of this ongoing work on each company's servers while providing himself with details of the progress of the work also constitutes *written memos* with the meaning of Birks and Mills (2015). Such written memos provide an effective and accurate resource for tracing the development of ideas, while also providing the researcher with accurate records for dissertation defense and future related research.

Storyline

The storyline strategy is a narrative device employed to aid in analysis within the systematic methodology of grounded theory. Storyline in the context of this dissertation has a double function: 1) assists in the production of the final theory; and 2) provides a means of clear conveyance to the reader (Birks & Mills, 2015). A tentative third unofficial function is that storyline literary device adds a familiar formatting design of *a beginning, a middle,* and *an end*. Plain English was deemed to work well to explain the overall findings of a grounded theory.

Participants, Institutional Review Board, and Ethical Concerns

Ethical concerns were a priority throughout the undertaking of this study. Adhering to the methods as outlined in this chapter was key to ensuring the legitimacy of this study.

This was a purely theoretical study. This study involved no human participants. The literature itself constituted the data for this research. Because this study involved no human participants, there existed no risks to participants; thus, no institutional review board was deemed necessary. Because no institutional review board was necessary, no institutional review board was convened. Regarding the research itself, there were no apparent ethical issues. Efforts to determine the ethical acceptability of research were undertaken and none were found.

Summary

The purpose of this chapter was to provide a detailed overview of the research methodology appropriately chosen for this *type* of research question. A discussion of the essential methods, study participants, data collection, and the specifics as to how the study itself was conducted.

Grounded theory was presented as the appropriate methodology; the process used to analyze the data from the 23-existing consciousness theories was detailed. There are three levels of analysis: initial coding; intermediate coding; and advanced coding. Constant comparative analysis was performed at each level of analysis; until themes emerged from the data.

Findings

The purpose of this chapter is to provide a transparent view of how the researcher used the findings of the research phase of this study to generate a novel theory. This study was a search for the "building blocks" to a *foundation of understanding* upon which to generate an original theory: an answer to the hard problem of consciousness.

This was a grounded theory study; therefore, *the storyline technique* was utilized as a strategy to present the findings clearly and logically. There were three levels of analysis: first, initial coding and categorization of data; second, the intermediate coding and identification of core categories; and third, advanced coding and theoretical integration. Steps were taken to explain exactly how the grounded theory methodology was applied to the *discovery* of, and *creation* of, this originally proposed holoplexity theory.

The Goal of the Research:
The Research Question

Does sufficient data exist in the literature upon which to predicate *and* generate an original, empirically compatible, nonreductive theory of consciousness sufficient to answer the hard problem of consciousness? It is important to note that this is a search for concepts that can then be combined in a meaningful way, and further combined with a new concept or concepts to create a new and viable theory to account for the hard problem of consciousness.

Data Collection

Consciousness is a vast interdisciplinary subject area. As this subject is already enormous while becoming larger every day, and because there are so many new and developing theories that are not explicitly distinct from their parent category of theory—a method of discrimination was deemed necessary. This study utilizes established theories that met certain criteria by searching for specific characteristics within both the theories themselves and within the literature. The specific criteria were the characteristics of being firmly *established* in the literature and published preferably in book form. These criteria led to the theories which had survived peer scrutiny and other judgment over time.

This method of discrimination was chosen as a data collection strategy because it was thought that the theories which had survived to this level of expression may be presumed to contain "enduring conceptual characteristics" worthy of examination. Such characteristics are thought to be appropriate for any search for the foundational knowledge of consciousness.

No researcher begins research with an empty slate and this researcher was no exception, having already read several books on "consciousness" as well as several "consciousness-related" books. The understanding that consciousness is an interdisciplinary topic was relatively new to academia; the process of discrimination started by ordering two popular *textbooks* on consciousness and a companion handbook to provide a broad overview of the interdisciplinary field. Two contemporary textbooks as well as a contemporary handbook would provide a comprehensive overview or framework of the entire interdisciplinary field of consciousness studies. The inquiry expanded from there.

Twenty-two (22) theories (and/or theory-clusters) of consciousness were ultimately selected to sufficiently represent the breadth and depth of consciousness studies that existed in the literature at the time of data collection. One (1) theory was discovered and added to those 22 theories upon further research into the quantum nature of consciousness itself, for a total of 23 theories. The main consideration associated with the concept of *sampling*, within this *qualitative* inquiry, was the notion of "saturation," as opposed to "representativeness" or "statistical sample size" (Neuman, 2003). Saturation occurs when incidences of a theme being to repeat within the research. *Purposive sampling* (Silverman, 2000) was utilized. The specific theories or theory clusters were selected on the criteria that they contained many of the concepts and characteristics found relevant or supportive within this study.

Data and Analysis

This section explains in detail the evolution of the data, beginning with the initial coding and categorization of the data. Once initial coding and categorization of the data were complete, intermediate coding and the identification of core categories were performed, and advanced coding and theoretical integration methods were applied.

Importantly, the method of "concurrent data generation" was combined with the "strategy of constant comparative analysis," as driven by "theoretical sampling" and utilized throughout this study. The activities of this *evolving analysis* were documented by the strategy of "memo writing" and this process was made transparent by the "storyline technique" method of presentation.

Initial Coding and Categorization of Data

Recalling that this is the first step of data analysis, initial coding and categorization of data is a method of identifying concepts of significance in the data and then *labeling* them for future use. *In vivo* codes are typically verbatim quotes from participants and are themselves sometimes used as labels. A *category* is a group of related codes. Categories are said to be *saturated* when additional data analysis returns codes that only appropriately fit into *existing* categories. Such categories should be sufficiently defined in terms of their properties and limits.

For this study, an example of this first step is seen in the initial dichotomy of theories that separated approaches to thinking about consciousness into *empirically based* and *theoretically based* approaches. This separation is significant because of the underlying *assumptions* that are implicit within each approach.

"Empiricism" imposed significant restrictions upon what was considered in the quest for understanding consciousness. That significant restriction was the *third-party observation* limitation. *Theoretically based*, which could easily have been also named *philosophically based*, was under no such restriction and therefore had greater degrees of freedom to explore that nature of that which was not fully understood. The term *theoretical* was chosen over the term *philosophical* because the presumed end goal of all these theories was to provide an adequate explanation of its subject matter of consciousness. Such an explanation would come with the implication of expanding the understanding of the metaphysics of reality—for all purposes, including scientific. Thus, the term *theoretical* was seen as something useful within—and common to—both the disciplines of science and philosophy.

It made sense to code and categorize the data concerning *the hard problem of consciousness* from the outset. Except that within the literature, it was not clear at this stage whether consciousness was determined to be a uniquely human phenomenon. *The hard problem of consciousness* was expressed in only human terms (in terms of "experience"), but the question itself was necessarily interpreted by the researcher not to be limited to human beings. It was read to be an open-ended question. The initial coding and categorization of the data were taken into consideration when addressing these preliminary questions.

Theories tangential to the hard problem

Several representative theories were determined to be too specific, too general, or too circumscribed in scope relative to the search for experience or consciousness (see Carruthers, 2017; Hameroff & Penrose, 1996; Lamme, 2006; Prinz, 2017; Seager & Bourget, 2017; Strawson, 2017; Varela, 1995; Zeki, 1999). Some theories were largely excluded by a single factor or multiple criteria while some portion or some aspect(s) of the theory(-ies) may still be included in the "findings" section of this study (see Carruthers, 2017; Eccles, 1994; Strawson, 2017). Partially relevant to this distinction were the differences between "hard" and "easy" problems of consciousness. This distinction will become clearer later, but some insight will be given here.

Theories were excluded if they tended to focus on the "easy problems" (Chalmers, 2017b, p. 364) of consciousness. According to Chalmers, *easy problems* include: (1) the ability to discriminate, categorize, and react to environmental stimuli; (2) the integration of information by a cognitive system; (3) the reportability of mental states; (4) the ability of a system to access its own internal states; (5) the focus of attention; (6) the deliberate control of behavior; and (7) the difference between wakefulness and sleep. A heuristic way of making this distinction is—the "easy problems" are those problems that tend to lend themselves to the existing standard methods of scientific inquiry. The hard problem of consciousness is *hard*— precisely *because* it does not lend itself to the existing methods of scientific inquiry.

Theories that deny consciousness

Consciousness was denied by some theories and theorists on various empirical or scientific grounds (Crick & Koch, 1990, 1994; Damasio, 1996, 1999; Edelman & Tononi, 2000; Llinas, 2002). Koch, regarding consciousness in a published interview, clearly stated that he believed subjectivity was *out of the purview* of science (Koch, 1992, italics added). Damasio admitted to his skepticism that science will find an answer to the hard problem of consciousness and purposefully delimits his theory to reflect this. Edelman and Tononi stated that they do not believe consciousness is an *object*, but rather a process. Llinas clearly stated that he does not believe that consciousness exists outside of the nervous system function.

　　Consciousness was otherwise denied by some theories or theorists by being re-identified, re-labeled, or re-named as something else (Hameroff & Penrose, 1996; Seager & Bourget, 2017; O'Regan & Noe, 2001; Varela, 1995; Zeki, 1999). Quantum theories were generally limited to theories of "mental causality" in which the attributes of quantum mechanics were thought to contribute significantly as such; they were too *functionally-focused* theories and did not tend to answer the hard problem of consciousness. Modern representationalism by Seager and Bourget was found to be more of "*an approach* to information processing" within the brain, than a full-blown theory of consciousness; thus, it was too narrow in scope to answer the broader question of how information becomes an experience and/or its explicit relationship to consciousness.

O'Regan and Noe, in sensorimotor theory, did not deny consciousness as a phenomenon but limited their theory of it to aspects attendant with awareness. Varela, in neurophenomenology theory, emphasized the primacy of consciousness but limited his theory to *an approach* to the empirical and methodological issues associated Zeki's microconsciousness theory is an interesting *discovery* that may turn out to be objectively verifiable, but as written it offers little to any greater understanding of the overall hard problem of consciousness.

Consciousness was implicitly denied by some theorists who reduced it to a kind of *functionalism* (Dretske, 2012; Lamme, 2006; Lehar, 2003; Metzinger, 2009; Prinz, 2017; Rosenthal, 2012; Vision, 2017). Dretske and Rosenthal are Higher-Order Thought (HOT) theorists who hypothesized that consciousness can be explained by, or reduced to, the interactive *function* of a higher-order state over a lower-order state. Lamme's theory of recurrent processing tends to reduce consciousness to neural *functioning*. Lehar and Metzinger are virtual reality (VR) theorists; VR theories tend to *limit consciousness* to the confines of the brain. Prinz's intermediate-level theory of consciousness was *too circumscribed* as to the exact location of where human consciousness seems to materialize while merely assuming the existence of consciousness itself. Vision, in emergentism theory, simply created a new ontological category for consciousness as emergent from neuronal interaction, while not addressing how this might occur.

Consciousness was even denied outright as *illusory* by some theorists (Dennett, 1991; Rosenthal, 2004, 2012). Dennett famously *explained away* consciousness in his book *Consciousness Explained* (1991) stating that there exists a kind of "fame in the brain" in which one draft of information takes primacy over other competing drafts, instead of consciousness. In 2004, Rosenthal joined Dennett in concluding that phenomenal consciousness was merely illusory.

Theories that recognize consciousness

A handful of theories and theorists do not deny the primacy of the ontology of consciousness (Baars, 2005; Bohm, 1980; Carruthers, 2017; Chalmers, 1995, 2017b; Dehaene, 2014; Strawson, 2017;

Tononi, 2004; Velmans, 1990, 2008, 2017a). Baars' and Dehaene's global workspace theories both begin and end with observable phenomena in the brain; thus, it was stated by Baars that *the hard problem does not apply*. However, this is not viewed as outright denial of the ontology of consciousness, but rather a reflection of the limitation of methods chosen, and the fact that Baars and Dehaene are concerned with human consciousness and not consciousness in isolation. Bohm's implicate order theory begins with the primacy of the ontology of consciousness itself and it is matter and mind (human consciousness) which extend from there. Like the global workspace theorists, Carruthers has a circumscribed dual-content theory that does not include consciousness in isolation, but rather with consciousness as found within the human brain. Chalmers admits within his naturalistic dualism theory to having *at least one missing nonreductive ingredient* toward an adequate explanation of consciousness while prescribing for the attributes of such a missing extra ingredient. Strawson's theory of physicalist panpsychism is a theory of consciousness itself, rather than of human consciousness. Tononi's information integration theory is essentially a mathematical description of *experience*, and as such is already presumably formatted from within the dual-aspect format of the bit. Velmans' reflexive monism theory is a reformulation of an ancient monistic theory that indicated that consciousness itself is more pervasive than commonly thought.

Summary of Initial Coding

This stage of inquiry eliminated theories that more explicitly denied the existence of consciousness as a phenomenon. Also, eliminated were theories that tended to deny *consciousness itself* more implicitly by attempting to reduce, rename, or equate it with mere brain function. The word *mere* is a key word here because brain function does appear to have an important role to play, but consciousness itself is very unlikely to be reducible to it.

Initial coding and categorization of the data tended to indicate that an answer to the hard problem of consciousness would not be found in limiting the inquiry to consciousness as found within the human brain. Understanding the *spirit of* the question of the hard problem of consciousness—as opposed to its denotative or literal meaning—meant that any real, non-reductive answer would lie beyond the boundaries of the human brain.

The results indicated that *consciousness itself* is a category and is larger than *human consciousness* as a category. Interestingly, *the hard problem* as a research question would appear to involve *both* categories. This further indicated that any answer was likely to involve proposed solutions to both sub-questions: (1) regarding the metaphysical nature of *consciousness itself*; and (2) regarding how the human brain interacts with *consciousness itself* to create the *human consciousness* that humans experience.

Intermediate Coding and
Identification of a Core Category

Intermediate coding is the second major stage of data analysis. Individual categories are developed by connecting sub-categories to fully develop their range of properties and dimensions. Next, the categories are linked together. Initial coding may be thought of as breaking down the data, whereas intermediate coding may be thought of as re-organizing the data in conceptually abstract ways.

For this study, the term *coding* is largely synonymous with *naming, describing*, or *identifying*. But more than that, it is naming, describing, or identifying a phenomenon as *specific to a distinct level of analysis*. Often, there is no substantive difference, except for the level of analysis. Remembering the example of water—at one level it is a molecule symbolized as H-O-H; at another level, it may be a droplet of rain; at another, it may be a glass of water; at yet another, it may constitute a cloud; at perhaps its largest level it constitutes about 71% of the Earth's surface. The point here is that each level is specific as to the level of *ability to analyze* the same substance (water). In other words, researchers would not use a Doppler radar to examine how molecules of water crystalize into ice, nor would researchers use a microscope to examine tons of water forming into storm clouds. Different levels of analysis require different kinds of analysis.

This study examines consciousness and proposes it *as* the foundation of reality. *Intermediate coding* represents a kind of coordination in describing and determining *where in the analysis* consciousness exists, as it is being described.

Initial coding led to a working hypothesis that *consciousness itself* was something that existed *independently of* human beings and their experience of human consciousness. Initial coding, therefore, led to a second working hypothesis that somehow the human brain can apprehend, or otherwise interact with, this "brain-independent" phenomenon—and utilize it. Thus, the focus changed to: What is the relationship of "consciousness itself" to "human consciousness?" Or, in other words, how does "human consciousness" come from "consciousness itself?"

The following related subcategories are a *chain of possible events* that were partially surmised from the data contained within both the literature review and initial coding processes. This chain forms a kind of pathway—which itself is composed of seven (7) sub-categories that link together in a logical and conceptually coherent manner. The seven subcategories can be thought of as seven-sub theories. Each of the seven sub-theories is individually grounded in the literature.

Core subcategory 1:
Consciousness as inherent within reality

It is hypothesized here that consciousness is *the singular* underlying dimension of reality. This proposition is inferred, in part, from the uncertainty principle as established by physicists Erwin Schrodinger (1925) and Werner Heisenberg (1927). This principle proposed that a particle/wave is indeterminate as far as position and velocity are concerned until *measured*. Proposing the trade of *consciousness* for *measurement*, two things may be surmised: (1) the direction of time; and (2) the onset of *time* as a phenomenon. Time is currently commonly thought to be the fourth dimension, but this is an unlikely scenario. Why? Because *time* appears to be a *function of*, or a byproduct of, consciousness itself (as *measurement*) combined with its own interaction with particle/waves (itself). Thus, it hypothesized that *consciousness*, not time, constitutes one of the four common dimensions of reality, with time again being a byproduct of these 4-

dimensions (Bohm, 1980; Hameroff, 2003). The other 3-dimensions are examined next.

The proposition that consciousness itself is a dimension of reality has implications for the nature of consciousness as humans experience it. It likely means that consciousness itself is irreducible. It also likely means that consciousness itself may have an independent expression within the underlying reality as experienced by humans. Human beings experience three dimensions (3-D) and *time*, but only *after* it has occurred (Bohm, 1980; Klemm, 2014; Sherrington, 1906; Singer, 2017). This is hypothesized to occur within the larger, primary, singular dimension of consciousness itself—which is proposed to be *timeless* within itself. This is a somewhat radical idea.

Regarding the other 3-dimensions, it is hypothesized that "consciousness itself" is captured from the environment via the human senses (within the various forms of stimuli) (Zeki & Bartels, 1999). Such information is then *unfolded* by virtue of structural components within itself. These structural components are further hypothesized to be *inherent*. The idea that they are *inherent* was surmised from how 2-D information becomes 3-D information, via the juxtaposition in the brain of two streams of 2-D information resulting in a single 3-D experience (Carter, 2002). This proposed "unfolded" consciousness necessarily includes time as a byproduct of consciousness itself, as an inherent component (Bohm, 1980). "Consciousness itself" is captured by human brain mechanisms. This will be described in greater detail later.

This core subcategory developed into the notion that "consciousness itself" acted as a primary, singular dimension in and of itself (a whole, or holo-). This core subcategory also partially contributed to the development of the idea that "consciousness itself" is a *plurality* (or -plexity), but significantly a *duality* at this and other levels of inquiry.

Core subcategory 2:
A temporary sentience
acquisition system in the brain

The existence of a temporary sentience acquisition system (TSAS) is hypothesized to exist in the brains of typically developing human infants. Sentience is defined as the *onset* and *ongoing experience of "self-awareness"* (Reber, Allen, & Reber, 2009, p. 717). The specific brain mechanisms which comprise the TSAS are not the specific focus of this study (however, they likely include the mirror neuron system, the infant internal body map, the temporary cross-wiring of the infant brain, the infant eidetic memory, and the two events of brain-pruning or apoptosis) (see Carter, 2002). As several of the mechanisms that comprise the TSAS are only *temporary* in development, it is further hypothesized that the TSAS exists for the *sole purpose of achieving sentience* in human infants *before* the onset of apoptosis.

This is a specific order of typical development that likely must occur before the neurodevelopmental milestone of *apoptosis* is maximally effective. Thus, this set of events constitutes a *sensitive period* in infant neurodevelopment; failure to develop in this area may result in atypical neurodevelopment, not unlike autism spectrum disorder (ASD).

This core category is the first of three which are integral in the hypothesis of how "consciousness itself" may be apprehended by human brain mechanisms.

Core subcategory 3:
Sentience develops into a concept of self

"Sentience" as a neurocognitive phenomenon, or a "concept," is likely then combined with ongoing consciousness or awareness activity to generate a neurocognitive *concept of self* (COS) (Klemm, 2014). The COS incorporates intellectual knowledge of "self-awareness" with bodily awareness (later developing into the separate sense of *proprioception*) (see Carter, Aldridge, Page & Parker, 2014). Along with additional knowledge and experience, the *theory of mind* develops (see Revonsuo, 2010). Because it is the amygdala (the hippocampus is not mature until approximately 2.5-years of age) that aggregates these neurocognitive concepts with sensory stimuli, it is hypothesized that the concept of self has a *deeply personal feel* attached to it (see Carter, 2002). Damasio (1999) referred to level as "core consciousness." The narrative phenomenological "I" is synonymous with the neurocognitive COS (and the embodied "I").

This core subcategory is the second of three (2 of 3) in a process that was hypothesized as integral to understanding how human brain mechanisms likely apprehend "consciousness itself." This neurocognitive phenomenon is likely what Carruthers (2017) hypothesized as the "mind-reading or theory-of-mind faculty, which has available to it concepts of experience, and which can access perceptual input." (p. 294).

Core subcategory 4:
COS develops into a central organizing mechanism (COM) of the brain and brain

The COS continues to develop over the lifespan; it is more commonly known to us as our narrative and phenomenological "I." However, once the COS is sufficiently neurodevelopmentally developed, it is hypothesized that the neurocognitive COS then becomes "encoded into" *all memories created* (Carter, 2002). This is key. The COS is proposed to be encoded into *all subsequent* incoming sensory streams and their products (see Klemm, 2014). Being encoded into all memories created is synonymous with becoming an element of those memories (Carter, 2010). Memories then become retrievable by their constituent elements (see Carter, 2010). As the COS is encoded into *each* memory, it ultimately becomes retrievable by the COS *primarily*. (This neurocognitive development may account for the universal phenomenon of "infantile amnesia.") Thus, the COS becomes the central organizing mechanism (COM) of the brain. The COM ties together memories across time and integrates them with the here-and-now. This makes sense as we phenomenologically recall "ourselves" as the subject and narrator of our pasts.

This is the third of three (3 of 3) in a neurocognitive process. These developmental mechanisms within this neurocognitive process are hypothesized to explain how human brain mechanisms can apprehend and make use of "consciousness itself." Upon being apprehended by these neurocognitive mechanisms, "consciousness itself" becomes "human consciousness" (as it is now a possession of the human brain). These three neurocognitive processes provide a conceptual direction and lead to the notion of a neurocognitive-electromagnetic link.

Core subcategory 5:
Overlapping brain systems create an emergent interface

First, an analogy may be useful here: the redundant sensory systems of vision, olfaction, and audition, which are *redundant and overlapping*, create an emergent property that is not found in any of the individual systems that combined to create it (Carter, 2010, 2014). "Emergent properties are the novel properties that arise when a higher level of complexity is reached by putting together components of lower complexity" (Capra, 2019, p. 154). The human visual system is likely the best example, although this emergent phenomenon exists in the auditory and olfaction systems also (Carter, 2002).

The visual system is comprised of two separate eyes with space or distance between them that feed simultaneous, overlapping stimuli to the brain. From these simultaneous, overlapping stimuli arises the emergent property of *depth perception*. Depth perception is *not an inference* of depth, as in parallax, but *an actual perception of depth* (Carter, 2010). Depth is the third dimension of 3-D. Thus, it can be said that the human sensory systems capture 2-D information at this level and 3-D information *emerges* from it.

It is hypothesized that the phenomena of *blindsight, blindsmell, blindtouch, reflex operations, the reticular activating system, REM sleep, the fight-flight response,* and *the Libet experiment* (1985) *all* tend to indicate the existence of still-operational ancient sensory systems (Carter, 2010; Klemm, 2014). These ancient systems are thought to operate *in conjunction with* the modern human sensory system today. Combined with the bilateral structure of the brain, this creates conditions for a multiple, dynamic overlapping system of inputs (see Klemm, 2014; 2019).

It is further hypothesized that these overlapping systems are separated, not only by position (space or distance) but also by distinct function and staggered in time. Again, analogous to and illustrated by the above example—this spatial and temporal separation of systems gives rise to the emergent property of dynamic 4-D consciousness property not found in any of the underlying but overlapping systems.

The more ancient sensory systems get stimuli to general *awareness* in approximately .1-second (Blackmore, 2004; Carter, Aldridge, Page & Parker, 2014). The modern human sensory system transforms stimuli to *self-awareness* in approximately .5-seconds (Blackmore, 2004; Carter, Aldridge, Page & Parker, 2014). It is believed that *human* consciousness as experienced, in its evolving 4-D form, exists in and emerges from this continuing, dynamic .4-second timeframe/overlap. The "brain's three minds" (Klemm, 2014; 2019) essentially pass the thought around between them, changing it; comprehending it; then immediately changing it again. Dehaene (2014) similarly stated, "Consciousness lives in the loops: reverberating neuronal activity, circulating in the web of our cortical connections, causes our conscious experiences" (p. 156). This dynamic, recursive brain activity has been theorized by thinkers from Sherrington in 1906 to Singer in 2017 and Klemm in 2019.

This is the core subcategory that led to the hypothesis that the architecture of reality unfolds from consciousness itself via this dynamic brain overlapping structure and multiple processes. Recall that this entire overall process has "consciousness itself" being *unfolded* from within itself (as stimuli)—while simultaneously the overall process is happening within the larger dimension of consciousness itself (because the brain exists within consciousness itself)—creating a kind of neurocognitive-electromagnetic linkage.

Core subcategory 6:
A new explanatory bridging principle

Holoplexity theory conceives of "human consciousness" as the *phenomenological experience of* mind-body "interface" connecting with the dimension of "consciousness itself." The first part of the two-part interface is explained here.

A robust kind of human consciousness must be established and must not be a mere epiphenomenon. More, that robust human consciousness must do more than mere "read" apprehended stimuli. It somehow interacts with it in some unexplained dynamic way that reflects our established reality. Such a dynamic interaction must also account for the phenomenal projection mystery as explained within the theory of reflexive monism. It must also account for the phenomenon of "human consciousness" appearing to satisfy the "measurement" criteria found within quantum theory experiments. This is the first part of that two-aspect "interface."

Rita Carter (2002) used the term "emergent macro-state" to describe this kind of state:

> [S]uppose that consciousness is an emergent macro-state that not only has different properties from the micro-states that give rise to it (as water has a different property, wetness, from its constituents) but that it also has different causal effects which "play back down" to the micro level. So unconscious brain state (or process) X produces conscious state A which has the power to change brain state X into brain state X1 which then produces conscious state A1 – and so on. In other words, once it has emerged consciousness becomes its own creator – no longer dependent on the senseless mechanisms that gave rise to it. (p. 68)

Further, Carter (2002) stated: "If consciousness state A is simply physical brain state X (i.e., they are identical) then there is no problem because one physical state can – in an ordinary way – affect another" (p. 69). Carter labeled and explained this specific kind of emergence: "In Emergence 2, consciousness does create itself by affecting the physical states from which it emerges. But to explain this downward causation we seem to require some *new explanatory bridging principal* [sic]... (p. 73; italics added)."

It is very noteworthy that not only Carter, but also McGinn, Chalmers, Velmans, and others all specifically make mention that something is missing from their respective theories. The "new explanatory bridging principle" is proposed here. It is the COS in conjunction with the imposition of the COM that coordinates the mental activity within the brain and mind.

The "downward causation" (Carter, 2002, p. 73) language or question is badly worded because the word *causation* is misleading and because it suggests two separate phenomena (i.e., the first *causing* the second). The conscious mechanisms embodied in thinking (neurocognitive symbols) are not separated from what they represent (see "perceptual projection" by Velmans, 2017). In essence, they *are* what they represent. Thus, it follows that when changes are made to their neurocognitive expressions, those changes are also manifest in their biological and neurophysiological expressions *because they are not separate*.

Very interestingly, Klemm (2014) used superficially different language to explain an essentially similar "explanator bridging principle":

A link between different levels of consciousness and distinct brain wave patterns has implications. First, and perhaps most profoundly, these observations suggest there is a continuous spectrum of consciousness, reflected in a continuous spectrum of different brain wave patterns. *This confirms the link between mind and matter*, although it cannot answer the age-old question: which came first, consciousness or the brain? (p. 107, italics added)

Again, Klemm (2014), putting it another way, stated essentially the same thing as indicated by Carter in 2002, and as described within this theory:

The code, because it arises from materialistic CIP [circuit impulse pattern] processes is an essential part of the machinery of the mind. The code can therefore influence the very circuitry from which it is being generated. This is key. *Read it again*, if necessary. In that way, a code in real-time can change the nature of the code at some future time. (p. 150, italics added)

The "code" as described by Klemm (2014) is synonymous with the concept of self (COS) (alternatively conceptualized as a code by Klemm) being encoded into incoming stimuli streams and all other products of the mind, thereby creating the self's central organizing mechanism (COM).

The researcher Bohm (1980) also explained the phenomenon on a more micro level. He explained that an electron has two aspects, the field aspect, and the particle aspect. The field aspect contains "active information" which guides the behavior of the particle aspect (Pylkkanen, 2006). In a phenomenon called "back action" (Sarfatti, 1997), it is thought the particle *can reciprocally affect its field.* This is a key concept.

This core subcategory is the first of two (1 of 2) subcategories to be combined to hypothesize the existence of the "mind" as a novel interface with the larger "consciousness itself." These two subcategories *combined* are thought to address the questions of "consciousness as measurement" conjecture and the "perceptual projection" mystery.

Core subcategory 7:
The Mind as the emergent macro-state
"interface" with consciousness itself

This is the second of the two-part (2 of 2) hypothesis which tends to address the questions of "consciousness as measurement" and the mystery of "perceptual projection."

Holoplexity theory tentatively provides the *new explanatory principle* to which Carter (2002) and others presumably referred. Specifically, the new principle is described conceptually via its mechanisms of the neurocognitive COS, or the embodied "I," interacting within the multiple operating systems, and as being imposed into existing stimuli, sensations, and thoughts, within an evolving, recursive nature of developing thought-building process, by additional multiple inputs, occurring within the proposed evolving .4-second time gap/overlap (aka COM).

The emergent "mind" (as an electromagnetic interface) is hypothesized to connect to the dimension of "consciousness itself" via its electromagnetic nature, its internal unfolding of the features of consciousness, and its external connection to the larger dimension of consciousness itself, within which *everything* exists).

This core subcategory is the second of two subcategories to be combined to form an interface with the larger dimension of consciousness itself. Consciousness itself as a duality, combined with *back action*, is the hypothesized conceptualization of how consciousness itself can interact with and connect to human brain mechanisms at the electromagnetic level.

Holoplexity theory hypothesizes the missing "extra ingredient," or "hidden aspect" is the *neurocognitive-electromagnetic linkage* to the larger (temporally hidden) "dimension of consciousness itself." It is proposed that this neurocognitive-electromagnetic interface has the nonlocal effects typically associated with the electromagnetic (electromagnetic fields), but further that the interface/link exists within the larger consciousness itself—thereby creating real connections within this non-spatial, non-temporal dimension.

Analysis and Synthesis

T he purpose of this qualitative grounded theory study is to generate an original, empirically compatible, nonreductive theory sufficient to offer a viable answer to the hard problem of consciousness. This chapter synthesizes and discusses the findings concerning the research question, the literature review, and the conceptual framework. Within the grounded theory framework, it is recommended that the findings *first* be presented in isolation from existing theories and the literature, then *secondly* be examined with the literature (Birks & Mills, 2015).

The nature of this research is purely theoretical. It seeks to examine existing theory to create new theory. Therefore, it is not always possible to completely separate the new theory from the existing theory, because it is not completely separate, as conceptual mechanisms tend to overlap and compete for explanatory efficacy, thereby bringing their origins into significance. However, what is possible is to give a kind of "before and after" contrast. And that is what was done here. In addition to this contrast, "Finding patterns and *themes* is one result of analysis" (Bloomberg & Volpe, 2016, p. 10, emphasis added).

The *findings* are essentially the parts or "themes" of a larger theory. Therefore, they may lose implicit meaning when presented in isolation. To remedy this potential loss, the parts (findings) will be presented as a whole (theory) first. Secondly, the parts, now identified as "themes," will be examined with the data or the literature. Keeping in mind that this is a grounded theory study, extra care will be taken in relating the parts or "themes" relate to the literature/data from which they are taken and by which they are grounded.

Here, the "before and after" contrast is flipped and is used as an analytical mechanism. The resulting theory is the "after," but is given *first* to illustrate the flow of information in the logical coherence of the newly generated theory. Presenting in this way preserves (by providing) the implicit "why" of each part (which constitutes the themes) in the overall newly generated theory. This recursive strategy is an integral part of the grounded theory methodology and is made explicit here.

A Necessary Reframing and Clarification of the Research Question

The hard problem of consciousness was originally posed as a question regarding *human consciousness*. That question can also be understood as reframed by Chalmers (1995; 2005; 2017a) and paraphrased here: *How does information become experience?* Integral to the understanding of this question are two points of clarification. First is that *information* is conceived of as a manifestation of *consciousness itself*, as communicated first by Wheeler (1980) and metaphysically interpreted by Chalmers (2017b). The second is that *experience* is understood to be a *human phenomenological event*.

In the reframing of the question, *consciousness itself* is seen both as existing independently of the human brain and as becoming apprehended by the human brain to become *a human experience* or *human consciousness*. The research question for this study was then approached as reframed and understood here.

A Statement of the Proposed Theory

Holoplexity Theory: From Monism to Multiplicity as a Proposed Answer to the Hard Problem of Consciousness

In the search for an answer to the hard problem of consciousness, *consciousness itself* was ultimately proposed to predate the universe, as a necessary precondition. Also, "consciousness itself" as a phenomenon was found to be necessarily distinguished from "human consciousness" as a related but separate phenomenon. Consciousness itself is hereby proposed to be *the* underlying "primary" strongest sense of the word, and the most basic dimension of reality, underlying even the more commonly understood three dimensions (3-D) of height, width, and depth. Dimension here is defined as a structure of reality. The commonly understood 3-D dimensions were proposed to *inhere within* the larger, more basic structure of the primary dimension of consciousness itself. This dimensional primary consciousness will be referred to as *consciousness itself*. It is proposed that matter arises from consciousness itself and not vice versa. It is further hypothesized that it is the interaction of matter/energy (as contained within 3-D) *with and within* consciousness itself (as the primary dimension) that is the causal factor of time. The result is the physically evident *before and after* that humans phenomenologically perceive, and conceive of, as *time*.

*"Consciousness itself" as distinguished
from "human consciousness"*

This theory proposes that consciousness itself necessarily predates the universe. As such, it then logically predates human beings. It is further proposed the human brain mechanisms developed and adapted to what already exists in nature. It is proposed in this study that panpsychism seems to be the most likely accurate scenario. Thus, it is proposed that human brain mechanisms developed for, and were adapted to, the panpsychism that has always existed in nature. It is hypothesized that human body mechanisms capture (via the senses) forms of this panpsychism, apprehend and interpret their essences (via brain structures), and make use of the information within them (via the mind). Therefore, consciousness itself is distinct from human consciousness because human brains do **not** generate consciousness, but rather capture, apprehend, and make use of it, as a medium.

Having distinguished *consciousness itself* as distinct from *human consciousness*, proposed below are the *characteristics* of consciousness itself that make it amenable to becoming utilized by the human brain. These characteristics are supported by, and grounded in, the data.

Consciousness itself as a
"hidden" dimension of reality

Due to its non-apparent manifestation, being non-spatial and non-temporal, the researcher further proposes that the *primary dimension of consciousness itself* fits the *hidden aspect or principle* conjecture of McGinn (1995). Humans tend to have very limited conceptual knowledge that is *independent of time*; thus, it is very difficult to generate an image (and even more difficult to create or write about an image).

Recall that according to holoplexity theory, matter arises from consciousness and not vice versa. Because we live in the spatial world of matter and the world of time, this necessarily means that the interactions between matter and consciousness have *already occurred*. Human beings exist within the immediate aftereffects of this interaction. It is experienced as a moment in time. One moment in time followed by another moment in time creates the conception of time. This after-the-fact manifestation of our reality and the notion that change is continuously occurring on sub-microscopic levels necessarily means that its cause is "hidden" from us.

Consider that all time is defined by change. Change is essentially movement. Movement is proposed to be a reification of the *potentiality* of consciousness itself. In quantum physics, it is movement itself, as expressions of quantum fields, by which particles are defined.

The point of this section is that the proposed dimension of consciousness itself fits the description of the "hidden aspect" as hypothesized by McGinn and others. The author essentially agrees with Bohm's (1980) and Wheeler's (2000) conceptions of quantum reality, taken by the researcher to be at least partially synonymous with consciousness itself.

Consciousness itself as a multiplicity

Using abductive logic (and a mental strategy of conceiving of *consciousness itself* as a kind of *pure potentiality*), consciousness itself would then appear to necessarily possess characteristics that would enable it to be the dynamic phenomenon that human beings experience it to be. Consciousness itself as "pure potentiality" began as an intellectual stand-in heuristic when the researcher needed a "placeholder" to continue hypothesizing about other aspects of consciousness itself. However, eventually the heuristic "pure potentiality" (implying a featurelessness) was just plain adopted as an alternative description of consciousness itself. This conception is generally consistent with the "holomovement" conception of Bohm (1980) and the "quantum foam" conception of Wheeler (2000).

The multiplicity as including
the structure of reality (3-D)

Surmised from the well-established evidence that two overlapping streams containing 2-D information *upon integration* form an image containing 3-D information, it is hypothesized that the *structure of reality* is contained within the information itself as a manifestation of consciousness itself. Alternatively said, 3-D information exists *within* the 2-D information if the 2-D information is a facet of a 3-D formation in reality. This is thought to necessarily mean then that the 3rd dimension (of 3-D) exists *within* the 2-D information itself. This concept will be explained in greater detail in a later section.

The multiplicity as including
the duality of matter/energy

This idea is necessary and following the information-bit doctrine by Wheeler (1980):

> *It from Bit* symbolizes the idea that every item of the physical world has at its bottom—at a very deep bottom, in most instances—an immaterial source and explanation; that which we call reality arises in the last analysis from the posing of yes-no questions and the registering of equipment evoked responses; in short, that all things physical are information-theoretic in origin and this is a participatory universe. (p. 5)

The quote "all things physical are information-theoretic in origin" is important here. This quote essentially states that *all* matter/energy has a common origin. If we take consciousness, as "human consciousness," to be self-evident, then we are necessarily stating the existence of at least one duality—the duality between matter and consciousness. Existing scientific methods have established that energy and matter are different manifestations of the same thing (i.e., $E=MC^2$). These ideas are then intellectually consistent with the notions of panpsychism and dualism.

The juxtaposition of brain structures allows
for the architecture of reality to unfold

The phenomena of *blindsight, blindsmell, blindtouch, reflex operations, the reticular activating system, REM sleep, the fight-flight response*, and *the Libet experiment* (1985) *all* tend to suggest the existence of still-operational ancient sensory systems (Carter, 2010; Klemm, 2014). These ancient systems are hypothesized to continue to operate *in conjunction with* the modern human sensory system today. It is hypothesized here that these overlapping systems are separated, not only by position (space), but also by different functions, and slightly staggered *in time*.

By analogy to the previous paragraph, this spatial and temporal separation in systems gives rise to the emergent property of dynamic, 4-D consciousness (as with the current conception of time), a property not found in any of the underlying but overlapping systems. The fourth dimension here is defined as *time* (as time is currently understood). The ancient systems get stimuli to *awareness* in approximately .1-second (Blackmore, 2004; Carter, Aldridge, Page & Parker, 2014). The modern human sensory system gets stimuli to *awareness* in approximately .5-seconds (Blackmore, 2004; Carter, Aldridge, Page & Parker, 2014). It is hereby proposed that "human consciousness", in its evolving 4-D form, exists in and emerges from within this continuing, dynamic .4-second timeframe/overlap.

According to Klemm (2013), the "brain's three minds" essentially pass the thought around between them, changing it, comprehending it, then immediately changing it again. Dehaene (2014) similarly stated, "Consciousness lives in the loops: reverberating neuronal activity, circulating in the web of our cortical connections, causes our conscious experiences" (p. 156). These findings led to the hypothesis that the inherent architecture of reality is located within manifestations of consciousness itself as it unfolds/integrates over these dynamic brain structures. These dynamic brain structures with their electromagnetic energy are collectively also known as "the mind."

> *Unfolding occurs simultaneously within both*
> *the brain and the larger consciousness itself*

As this unfolding/integration occurs within human consciousness (the mind), the unfolding/integration is not separate from the larger *consciousness itself* because the mind exists, along with everything else in the world, within the larger dimension of consciousness itself. Human consciousness then establishes an automatic and immediate re-connection *to/with* consciousness itself as a dimension (aka reality).

The 3-D structure was hypothesized to be inherently contained within the *information* itself; therefore, the 3-D thought is *subjected to* and *within* the dimension of primary consciousness as it unfolds/integrates (thereby adding the fourth-D) in the human mind, making it a 4-D phenomenon (an active thought occurring *in time* within a connection to reality).

Recall that the dimension of consciousness itself is proposed to be non-spatial and non-temporal. Recall also, that this dimension is proposed to underlie all of reality and is proposed to be the primary underlying causal factor of time. If these conditions are true, then any given moment in time of this reality must be expressed in some form in this dimension (i.e., like photograph, blueprint, "glimpse", etc.). It is further proposed, given the underlying wholeness or oneness of the nature of reality, that human observation is an act of "consciousness itself" reflexivity and therefore constitutes a "real connection" within this realm. This realm is the non-spatial, non-temporal dimension of consciousness itself that *gives rise to* the reality that we humans know.

During unfolding/integration: An automatic
re-connection to the larger consciousness itself occurs

Consciousness itself here is manifested as *sensory information* which also exists within the larger consciousness itself; it then unfolds/integrates *into itself.* This is a difficult concept to convey, but the action of unfolding/integration *is not separate from* the action of reconnecting to the larger consciousness itself. **These are one and the same actions.** As this presumably occurs at an electromagnetic level, this is immediate, seamless, and automatic.

As mentioned in the previous section, human observation is made in the world. Therefore, it is necessarily "recorded" onto/into the non-spatial, non-temporal dimension of consciousness itself, thereby becoming reified in the world as demonstrated by the *double-slit experiments* in physics.

The reconnection to the larger consciousness itself
makes a human thought instantaneously a part of reality

Once this former sensory information is unfolded/integrated and reconnected to the larger consciousness itself, it has acquired the status of *existent* within reality. The term "existent" is a past-tense word and thus a function of time.

Thus, in short, consciousness itself (*as information*) entered the brain as sensory stimuli. It then was unfolded/integrated by the structure of the brain. Through the action of unfolding/integration, it became simultaneously reconnected to the larger consciousness itself. Its status now is that of a non-apprehended thought existent within reality. The final aspect of the proposed theory deals with the human brain's apprehension of that thought.

It is proposed that this model answers or constitutes the missing *extra ingredient* (Chalmers, 1996), the *hidden aspect or principle of space* (McGinn, 1995) the *new explanatory bridging principle* (Carter, 2002), and the *missing explanatory model* (Velmans, 2008), *the explanatory gap* (Levine, 1983), and *the binding problem* (Treisman, 1980).

Neurocognitive mechanisms apprehend
the unfolded consciousness itself

This is the point at which our neurocognitive concept of self (COS) can apprehend this thought and make it its own "possession." How does it do this? It is hypothesized that brain mechanisms (most likely the hippocampus [ordinarily] and the amygdala [in emergencies]) encode the COS into *all* incoming sensory streams/products. Something (COS) that is encoded into all memories that are created is synonymous with becoming an element of those memories at some level. Memories then become retrievable by virtue of their constituent elements (Carter, 2010). As the COS is encoded into *each* memory as it becomes retrievable by the COS *primarily*. "Primarily" here means that the COS becomes the central organizing mechanism (COM) of the brain. The COM ties together memories across time and integrates them with the here-and-now. (From this point forward, consciousness as found within the brain— are the problems which Chalmers (2017b) identified and defined as the *Easy Problems of Consciousness*.)

Discussion

Recalling that it is recommended in the grounded theory literature to begin with the findings first, then discuss them in contrast to their constituent theories (Birks & Mills, 2015), the findings (as components of the generated theory) are presented here, and the constituent sub-theories are discussed next, as prescribed. It is recommended that the reader have a general understanding of the novel theory to make meaningful the story of how the researcher came to those interpretations. However, the story of how the researcher came to his interpretations may help the reader to understand the novel theory itself.

Advanced Coding and
Theoretical Integration (Themes)

Recall that advanced coding, or the creation of *themes*, is integral to the idea of theoretical integration. As mentioned previously, advanced coding procedures include the use of *the storyline technique* to both integrate and present the resultant grounded theory. *Story* is defined as a descriptive narrative about the central phenomenon of the study, and *storyline* is defined as the detailed sequential delineation of how the theory came into existence. Theoretical codes, or themes, may be taken from existing theories to facilitate theoretical integration while adding explanatory power to the final product. This stage *also makes clear* the newly generated grounded theory's position within the existing body of knowledge. The final product is an integrated and comprehensive new grounded theory with explanatory power regarding a process or a scheme associated with a phenomenon.

For this study, the previous example of *consciousness as a dimension* is relevant to this step. *Time* as a phenomenon may seem tangential to the study of consciousness until one considers the depth of analysis. At the most basic level, *everything* will be relevant, as consciousness is proposed to be *the* underlying structure of *all reality*. If so, then consciousness must be somehow compatible with all other physical phenomena observed in nature. Time is one of those phenomena. Thus, if consciousness itself contains the underlying physical structure of reality, then the physical structure of existence must be *integrated* with consciousness itself. This proposed theory integrates these two phenomena.

How does *information* become *experience*? This is an *interpretation* or possibly a *simplification* and a *restatement* of the "hard problem of consciousness" by the philosopher and cognitive scientist David Chalmers. Through examination of the selected 23 theories of "consciousness" presented in the literature review; it became apparent to the researcher that the hard problem of consciousness was *not limited to human consciousness*. Instead, the hard problem necessarily extended to *consciousness itself* (consciousness that is outside of, or independent of, the human experience of consciousness). The literature tended to demonstrate that virtually all possible combinations of theory were elaborated upon without providing a satisfactory conceptualization of how *mere information* becomes a *human experience*.

What also became clear was that some researchers appeared to stop searching upon finding a seemingly sufficient explanation for *the hard problem*. Thus, these researchers began to reduce, rename, or otherwise identify human consciousness as merely a kind of human brain function. This apparent concession, of relegating consciousness to brain function, was intellectually unsatisfactory. Within the existing literature, one researcher distinguished himself as likely the most ardent proponent of *not* allowing the hard problem of consciousness to be relegated to something lesser. He is the philosopher and cognitive scientist David Chalmers.

It was at this point that greater focus was placed upon the theoretical framework of *the hard problem* as delineated by Chalmers. Chalmers indicated that there seemed to be a *missing extra ingredient* within current accounts of human consciousness, that rendered those accounts inadequate. In the quest for a satisfactory account and theory and given that this hard problem of consciousness has persisted for millennia despite the many types of available theories, this assessment of the field and literature seemed eminently reasonable.

Given that Chalmers' reframing of the hard problem of consciousness seemed to be *on point*, a closer examination of the ontological status of *information* seemed to be the next logical step in this search. Recall that Chalmers reframed the question by asking how *information* became *experience*. It was the pursuit of this knowledge regarding the ontological status of "information" that led the researcher outside the realm of "human consciousness" into the realm of "consciousness itself."

Theme 1:
Reality as Inherent within Consciousness Itself

Recalling that specific to grounded theory, as a research design, is the process of *concurrent data generation* in which samples are first purposefully chosen; from these samples, data are collected or generated. These data are then *coded* before additional data are collected or generated. This strategy, or process of analysis, is then generally *repeated.* It is this specific procedural step that tends to differentiate grounded theory from other types of research designs (Glaser & Strauss, 1967).

Within this study, this step in the process is perhaps *the most important single step* of systematic grounded theory methodology. One example of this step is the practice of actively discriminating the *significance* of what is being coded parallel to one pursuing the data. This is where and when the concept of *"recursive"* is used when applying data itself to the search for additional data. The *data* consists of existing theory, by considering the *conceptual implications* of each theory (or a part of the theory); such considerations implied a *conceptual direction* of where to look for further relevant data to advance the developing theory. As a more concrete example, if the metaphysical implications of the notion of *panpsychism* were pursued, then pursuing that in that conceptual direction would occur as opposed to the metaphysical implications and direction of the notion of *emergentism*. While good scholarship requires *both* implications to be thoughtfully *considered*, concurrent data generation requires only one to be actively pursued (to avoid the generation of parallel, but conflicting data). In this instance, both panpsychism and emergentism were necessarily pursued until one direction appeared stronger and more likely than the other (panpsychism). However, it is not that simple—as a level of analysis is very relevant— it turns out that *emergentism* has a role in "human consciousness" but not in "consciousness itself."

It is proposed in holoplexity theory that the underlying structure of reality may be found within consciousness itself. This is the *converse* of the proposition that was stated earlier in subcategory 1 of the intermediate coding phase. The elements of that proposition are reversed; because at its base, it is a singular, holistic entity. If it makes sense that "something" is "itself", then those two elements can be readily reversed and remain valid. This is mentioned here because the work is using the same *discovery*, but from a different perspective to gain additional insight.

This proposition that reality may be inherent within consciousness itself was inferred, again, from the uncertainty principle as established by physicists Schrodinger in 1925 and Heisenberg in 1927. This principle proposed that a particle/wave is indeterminate as far as position and velocity were concerned until measured. Proposing the substitution of "consciousness" for "measurement" (Chalmer 1996; London & Bauer (1939); Wheeler

& Zurek (1983); Wigner (1961)), two things may be hypothesized: (1) the direction of; and (2) the onset of *time* as a phenomenon. *Time* is currently commonly thought to be the *fourth dimension* of reality. However, this may not be so, because time appears to be an *effect* of, or the *result* of, consciousness itself (as measurement) interacting with particles/waves. Thus, it proposed that consciousness itself, and *not* time, is a more primary dimension of reality.

This proposition that reality exists within "consciousness itself" (as a dimension) has implications. It likely means that consciousness itself as a phenomenon is irreducible. It likely also means that the structure of reality is an expression of consciousness itself. Here again, we see that consciousness appears to be the "whole"—but a whole (holistic or holo-) that is differentiated into dimensions, structures, and matter/energy (multiplicity or -plexity). It is the overall interaction within this "whole" that creates the resultant effect of what humans perceive as "time."

Back to the inquiry into information, re-assembled "information" presumably includes *consciousness itself as an inherent component*, but this kind of consciousness has become "human consciousness" because it was regenerated and apprehended by human brain mechanisms. The re-assembled information from consciousness itself (now human consciousness) *amounts to an interface* within the dimension of consciousness itself during active integration; *integration* itself is thus a kind of "connection." The reassembled (human) consciousness does *not* exist outside of, or independent of, the primary dimension of *consciousness itself*. Human consciousness is proposed to be assembled within the larger dimension of consciousness itself, and is thus a part of it.

It is proposed that this unfolding and connecting of information, or *integration* of information, which occurs within the brain (which in turn exists within the larger *consciousness itself*) constitutes the *integration* of humanly-apprehended consciousness *with* consciousness itself. This is an important concept.

It is proposed and key to mention here that the human brain does not *integrate* the information; rather it merely *connects* the information. It is the information itself that is ever-changing, thereby creating the integration of its own expression. This was inferred from binocular (3-D) vision coming from two monocular (2-D) sources. This phenomenon does not occur in a bubble but is proposed to be a more accurate reflection of a reality that exists outside the human brain. Nowhere is a 3-D reality apprehended by any human apparatus, but it is from an *unfolding of the information itself* within the human brain that a 3-D reality is revealed.

This is the hypothesis of how *consciousness itself* (manifest as information) is gathered by human brain mechanisms (via the senses) and then assembled into human consciousness, by a reciprocal reconnection with the larger dimensional consciousness itself. An oversimplified, partial, analogy would be a common radio signal, gathered and reassembled. It is the continuously changing nature of the information itself that is captured that creates the music and *not* any manipulation by radio mechanisms. Human sensory information (containing consciousness/dimensional information) would be analogous to the radio signal. Meaning that once the information is reassembled and integrated, the connection is timeless, automatic, and instantaneous because it exists simultaneous to the underlying, primary dimension of consciousness itself. The consciousness itself that is contained within the "information" connects back to "primary consciousness itself" which comprises the dimension of reality. Sensory information is limited by what specific electromagnetic energies our human senses can gather, and by what our human bodies and our human brain mechanisms can interpret meaningfully.

Grounded indications

It appeared that the human senses capture something *already existent* in nature (i.e., 3-D). The researcher reasoned that the mechanisms of human consciousness likely developed for that same reason (to *apprehend and make meaningful* what already exists in nature). When the nature of what it is that was captured by the human senses was contemplated, it was hypothesized that these phenomena were more in the domain of physics (i.e., light, vibration, temperature, electromagnetism, etc.) than of any other field. What was also hypothesized was that whatever energy was gathered from the environment was then reconfigured into useful electromagnetic waves by the brain. It was further hypothesized that it was the activity of electromagnetism that was *key*. But why and how could this be? Still, these grounded indications provided a conceptual direction for the research.

While researching quantum theories in which it is postulated that all of existence may be predicated upon *possibility and probability*, the researcher combined the *idea* that time seems not to exist (except as posteriori) with the scientific thought experiment performed by Einstein that included a *ray of light* at the *speed of light*. What exactly was Einstein trying to ascertain about *light* while traveling *at the speed of light*? The researcher tentatively hypothesized that at the speed of light, light would be a kind of pure dichotomy—a kind of *pure potentiality*—both a photon *and* a wave, but *not* a photon or a wave separately (phenomenal *physical light* having been factored out, at the speed of light). This suggested insight into the idea that all of existence may be somehow predicated upon this holistic duality (within the holistic multiplicity).

Any such *question* begs the further question of a *beginning*. How did this come to be? How did it all start? These questions are still unanswerable, but the next best question was then posed: what was the *first* identifiable instance of this holo-duality? It seemed to the researcher that the Big Bang was likely the first *identifiable* instance and the first *before and after* a posteriori *definition of time*. There was a "before the Big Bang" and an "after the Big Bang," putting consciousness itself in existence *before* the Big Bang, given that is proposed that manifestations of consciousness itself were the constituent parts of the Big Bang (McGinn, 1995). The universe as we know it came into existence *after* the Big Bang.

Theme 2:
Consciousness Itself as the Primary Dimension

Within theoretical sampling, when it becomes apparent that additional information is required to *saturate* categories under development, a *strategic decision* is made about where to find specific compatible additional information to fulfill analytical needs. Theoretical sampling is the mechanism used to feed the process of constant comparative analysis. The key component of theoretical sampling is "saturation" and *not* representativeness; the size of the sample is *not* statistically determined.

Within this study, this step represents another *key* methodological distinction. Recalling the research question of whether sufficient data exists in the literature upon which to propose a *new* theory suggests then that this new theory must possess qualities not currently found in existing theories. This is most likely true; otherwise, there would be no need to search for, or to generate, a novel theory in an attempt to answer the hard problem of consciousness. This also means that current thinking, current theorizing, is likely somehow missing the mark. Going back to the *missing-keys metaphor* from chapter 1, the search is now directed to more unlikely places. Recalling that *representativeness* of something already deemed *more unlikely* will, *by definition,* tend not to be statistically abundant. Thus, under these circumstances and from the outside looking in, whatever theory generated will *necessarily appear* to have little theoretical conceptual support within the literature. However, in the time it took to conduct and write this study, that level of *conceptual support* appears to be changing. This is the *nature of* what is being sought by this study. Additional conceptual support appears to be accumulating as it becomes apparent where to look within the data (the literature).

The primary dimension here is defined as an irreducible singularity. The primary dimension is only intellectually distinct from the three commonly known structural dimensions of length, width, and depth (often described as 3-D), which are hypothesized subsumed within consciousness as the *primary* dimension. Again, this is how the network or multiple (*-plexity)* is hypothesized to come from the whole or one (*holo-*). What follows is the grounded conceptual support found within the data.

Grounded indication: Wheeler

According to *Wheeler* (1989) regarding "information," *the boundary of a boundary is 0* (or nothing). The universe is *something* or conceptualized here as 1. Recognizing that before the Big Bang could be interpreted as nothing or zero (or half of a *bit*), the creation of *something from nothing* suggested the onset of time (as well as the creation of the first *bit*); this further suggested that time was a *by-product* and not an irreducible thing, in and of itself. This illustrated the interaction between three intellectually separate things: two possibilities and consciousness itself. (They can only be said to *intellectually separate*, while in reality, they are one whole.)

In thinking that if there were nothing, then there would be no possibilities. Inherent in the word *possibilities* itself is the concept of time. This seemed to be more evidence that whatever causes time came before any *possibility* of possibility. Therefore, the researcher speculated that *whatever causes time* came before the creation of the universe. Thus, it was hypothesized that what caused the *choice* between 0 or 1—between the *universe* and *nothing*—was consciousness itself. During the study, the researcher found a report in which Hameroff (2003) came to essentially the same conclusion, but by parallel reasoning, stating, "Conclusion: Consciousness creates time" (p. 5). This specific conclusion was the only aspect of the Hameroff theory (as understood) that was found to be in accord with the proposed holoplexity theory. This is an example of separate aspects of various other theories seeming correct, but it is relevant only specifically to the question posed and to the *specific level of inquiry*. Understanding that some "truth" only exists at specific "levels of inquiry" is important to understanding this study.

Grounded indication: McGinn

McGinn (1989) proposed that due to cognitive limitations within human brains, humans will *never* grasp the nature of consciousness. However, later McGinn (1995) clarified his proposed human cognitive limitations; because it is *human consciousness* that humans use to pursue this understanding of *consciousness itself* that the limitation is thus inherent. In deciphering the mystery of the relationship between *humans* and their *personal experiences* (of consciousness), McGinn is likely mistaken as this endeavor seems promising. It is likely that humans can arrive at a satisfactory conceptual understanding of how *consciousness itself* is individually *experienced* within the human brain. Again, however, it is relevant and specific to the *question asked* because *if* it is reductive "scientific" *proof* that is sought, then McGinn is likely correct.

McGinn's (1995) work "grounds" this proposed theory well by the statement, "mind is no kind of out-growth of matter but an *independent ontological category*" (p. 5, italics added). Secondly, McGinn made a *critical* observation stating, "Things in space can generate consciousness only because those things are not, at some level, just how we conceive them to be; *they harbor some hidden aspect or principle*" (p. 6, italics added). Additionally, consciousness is not a "thing" (p. 2) in the sense of modern physics and that consciousness has a *non-spatial character*; further, "The realm of the mental is just not bound up in the world of objects in space in the way that ordinary physical events are so bound up" (p. 2). All of these *findings* by McGinn are very consistent with the proposed Holoplexity theory.

Grounded indication: Strawson

Strawson (2017) wrote an elegant 16-page philosophical proof regarding the concept of physical panpsychism that was coherent, compelling, and irrefutable. Strawson's physical panpsychism was defined as matching the *Oxford English Dictionary* type of theory in which "there is an element of consciousness in all matter" (p. 374). Strawson (2017) stated:

> I conclude that genuine, realistic monist naturalists ought to favor panpsychism above all other theories of the nature of concrete reality, on the grounds of theoretical simplicity and ontological parsimony (one can add in "Occam's Razor" as a further premiss). Everything true in physics remains in place, and physics continues to be a theory about the nature of concrete reality. (p. 387)

In thinking about all that exists—the researcher cannot help but notice that there seemingly needs to be a *staging area* for all of it. That staging area may be better described in terms of *dimensions*, the three (3) that humans can appreciate, and which are commonly referred to as 3-D. It was at this point that the researcher hypothesized, by the process of abduction, that consciousness is the larger underlying, *primary dimension*; from which the other 3-

dimensions must have to *"unfold"*. The researcher further hypothesized that it is the *interaction* that must have to occur among and between these 4-dimensions that creates the *effect* of the human experience of *time*.

Theme 3:
Consciousness Itself as a Multiplicity/Duality

For this theory, consciousness is hypothesized to be a holistic primary dimension from which the other 3-dimensions unfold. *Consciousness* itself is then further hypothesized to be structurally differentiated from *physical matter* at the human macro-level. Consciousness, then, exists as both: (1) as matter itself; and (2) as the structural architecture of reality. *This constitutes the multiplicity of consciousness, as well as the duality of matter.* This is also another way of restating the notions of "panpsychism."

Grounded indication: Wheeler

The *duality/multiplicity of consciousness* is somewhat difficult to comprehend and expound so other alternative and additional grounding (in the literature) seem to be useful here. One such alternative conceptualization, or perspective, is contained within the language of *Wheeler* (1980):

> *It from bit* symbolizes the idea that every item in the physical world has at bottom—at a very deep bottom, in most instances— an immaterial source and explanation; that which we call reality arises in the last analysis from the posing of yes-no questions and the registering of equipment-evoked responses; in short, that all things physical are information-theoretic in origin and this a *participatory universe.* (p. 5, italics added)

This is another grounded conceptualization of the proposed duality/multiplicity from the perspective of the *bit*, in information theory, as expressed within the reasoning of Wheeler.

Grounded indication: Maxwell

Further alternative conceptualization or perspective is provided within the language of *Maxwell* (1978):

> Even within the bounds of present physical theory, we might consider a fanciful but logically coherent possibility. Fields— electrical, magnetic, or gravitational—and fluctuations in fields are, *as far as their structures are concerned*, viable candidates for identification with (some kinds of) mental states or mental events. (p. 399)

This is a second grounded conceptualization of the same proposition of *duality or multiplicity*, alternatively conceptualized from the perspective of *fields*, in the words of Maxwell. The *duality/ multiplicity of consciousness* is readily seen here as synonymous with the *duality of matter*—again specific to a very, very deep level of inquiry.

Grounded indication: Chalmers

A third alternative conceptualization is further grounded in the descriptive language of *Chalmers* (2017b). This *double aspect* may be thought of as a *quality* that exists "as part of the basic furniture of this world" (p. 365). More specifically, Chalmers (2017b) stated:

> The double-aspect principle stems from the observation that there is a direct isomorphism between certain physically embodied information spaces and certain *phenomenal* (or experiential) information spaces... That is, we can find the *same* abstract information space embedded in physical processing and conscious experience. (p. 370)

Chalmers further speculated on the existence of the intrinsic and extrinsic properties of information. Chalmers (2017b) wrote:

> Once a fundamental link between information and experience is on the table, the door is opened to some grander metaphysical

speculation concerning the nature of the world. For example, it is often noted that physics characterizes its basic entities only *extrinsically*, in terms of their relations to other entities, which are themselves characterized extrinsically and so on. **The intrinsic nature of physical entities is left aside.** (p. 371, italics in text, bold added)

If this were the end of the quote, it would be largely unremarkable—except that it seems to indicate additional characteristics in evidence, somehow internally, intrinsically, or inherently. To the researcher, the intrinsic nature of physical entities is arguably the quantum aspect of them. Which again has an isomorphic similarity to the study of consciousness. What is remarkable is contained in the continuation of the above Chalmers (2017b) quote:

Some argue that no such intrinsic properties exist, but then one is left with a world that is pure causal flux (a pure flow of information) with no properties for the causation to relate. If one allows that intrinsic properties exist, a natural speculation, given the above, is that the intrinsic properties of the physical—the properties that causation ultimately relates—are themselves phenomenal properties. **We might say those phenomenal properties are the internal aspect of information.** (p. 371)

This speculation by Chalmers is strongly consistent with this theory. Recalling that the medium of the mind is thought to be electromagnetic and that environmental stimuli that human sense organs and relays to the human brain are electromagnetic (or immediately converted to electromagnetic information), it makes sense that an electromagnetic expression may be common across information and this is likely the medium of the phenomenal.

This is important because researchers, in general, seem to be looking for something other than the functional, leading to a belief that human consciousness is then a mere epiphenomenon. However, what Chalmers seems to be speculating and what this researcher believes is that "the phenomenal" is another aspect or facet of "the functional" as expressed and then realized *electromagnetically* via brain and mind mechanisms.

However, the news by Chalmers is not all good. Chalmers (2017b) finishes his quote with a highly plausible explanation and an admonition:

> This could answer a concern about the causal relevance of experience—a natural worry, given a picture on which the physical domain is causally closed, and on which experience is supplementary to the physical. The informational view allows us to understand how experience might have a subtle kind of causal relevance in virtue of its status as the intrinsic nature of the physical. This metaphysical speculation is best ignored for the purposes of developing a scientific theory, but in addressing some philosophical issues it is quite suggestive. (p. 371-72)

This part of the Chalmers quote is again quite consistent with the proposed theory. A 3rd dimension (of 3-D) was *hidden* in 2-D information until allowed to manifest via the dynamic structures of the brain and apprehended by the mind—the phenomenal facet of information is not apparent when information is considered only on its functional merits. However, only when information is *expressed* electromagnetically in "the mind" does its phenomenality become apparent. Electromagnetically is the medium of the mind, and the mind is how humans perceive phenomenally. If this is true, then epiphenomenalism is not a concern in this view of reality.

As the purpose of this study is to provide a broad conceptual understanding regarding "how information becomes experience," philosophical/metaphysical speculation seems especially salient because traditional "scientific methods" tend to preclude the kind of thinking that seems to be indicated by the questions inherent in "the hard problem of consciousness." Recall that the ontology of science had to be *expanded* in the nineteenth century to accommodate electromagnetic processes which could not be explained in the mechanical processes of the day. Electromagnetic charges and electromagnetic forces became new fundamental components of a physical theory at this time.

Grounded indication: Velmans

A fourth conceptualization, given here as a grounded alternative explanation, was found within the theory of *reflexive monism* as proposed by *Velmans* (2017a):

> In this monist vision, there is one universe (the *thing itself*), with relatively differentiated parts in the form of conscious beings like ourselves, each with a unique, conscious view of the larger universe of which it is a part. Insofar as we are parts of the universe that, in turn, experience the larger universe, we participate in a reflexive process whereby the universe experiences itself. (p. 361)

Arguably, this conceptualization begins with the notion that all is *one* and that *one is consciousness*. This is an alternative way of saying that the mechanisms of consciousness, and the information apprehended by those mechanisms, are *both composed of consciousness itself,* however, *differentiated.* Being composed of *one thing but differentiated* may be readily interpreted as a definition of a *multiple-* or *dual-aspect.* Again, the term "duality" has a valid meaning at specific levels of inquiry only (because on the most basic level, there is no duality).

Grounded indication: McGinn

Another alternative but parallel perspective regarding the unknown metaphysical aspects of the universe, *McGinn* (1995) said, "According to our earlier speculation, these aspects may be connected to features of the universe that played a part in the early *creation of matter and space itself*—those features, themselves pre-spatial, that characterised the universe before the big bang" (p. 7, italics added). However, McGinn (1995) concluded, "Clearly, *the space of perception and action* is no place to find the roots of consciousness. In that "sense" consciousness is not spatial, but we seem unable to develop a new conception of space that can overcome the *impossibility* of finding a place for consciousness in it" (p. 10, italics added).

Again, specific to the question posed (i.e., "roots") McGinn is right, but only because a singularity would, by definition, not have any roots. Ironically, it is the *space of perception and action* that gives rise the some of the most meaningful inferences of consciousness itself that are available to human beings (i.e., 3-D from 2-D visual information).

McGinn (1995) made further *key* observations, stating, "Things in space can generate consciousness only because those things are not, at some level, just how we conceive them to be; *they harbor some hidden aspect or principle*" (p. 6, italics added); that consciousness is not a "thing" (p. 2) in the sense of modern physics and that consciousness has a *non-spatial character*; and "The realm of the mental is just not bound up in the world of objects in space in the way that ordinary physical events are so bound up" (p. 2). This hidden aspect and the *generation of consciousness* notions tend to support the ideas of multiplicity, duplicity, and unfolding.

This concludes several examples, each grounded in the literature, that alternatively tend to illustrate the *duality/multiplicity of consciousness*. This aspect was conceived of as an integral part of the proposed human consciousness *interface*. The other integral part of the proposed human consciousness *interface* is the *duality of matter*. This needs to be stated explicitly because it is a central tenet of this proposed novel theory. It is the mechanism by which *the dimension of consciousness itself* interfaces with *the physical world* and *the consciousness of humans*.

For example, once an *individual human interface* connects to the *dimension of primary consciousness* and the information is received, apprehended, and interpreted—only then does it become human "experience" (as understood in Chalmers, 2017a, p. 33) as it is now a possession of its human physical mechanisms.

Since it was argued that humans cannot know *consciousness* independent of *experience* (see McGinn, 1995), *for the purposes of this study*, human experience will be regarded as fundamental to a specific level of inquiry. Regarding human experience as fundamental, Chalmers (2017b) stated:

Of course, by taking experience as fundamental, there is a sense in which this approach does not tell us why there is experience in the first place. But this is the same for any fundamental theory. Nothing in physics tells us why there is matter in the first place, but we do not count this against theories of matter. Certain features of the world need to be taken as fundamental by any scientific theory. (p. 364)

This concluded the search for evidence supporting the specific proposed constructs of consciousness itself as a dimension (primary) and further that consciousness itself as existing as a duality (within a multiplicity), and again interacting within itself, to create 4-D (also can be conceptualized as *3-D in time*).

Other grounded indications

The next part of this section is a search for the theoretical (meaning as concepts bound within a coherent theory) but sometimes provides conceptual grounded support. In other words, aspects of theories but not the entire theory itself can tend to add support despite the entire theory as a whole may run counter to the proposed new theory.

Although somewhat self-explanatory, it is important to remember that the *duality of matter* is distinct from, but a complement to, the *duality of consciousness*. Partially due to the very different ontological statuses of *matter* and *consciousness itself* in Western thought, this is necessarily repeated here. This distinction tends to be the crux of confusion, as well as the basis of Descartes' dualism. This idea is so *ingrained* in many people's minds that it is difficult for them to conceive otherwise.

Grounded indication: Dualism

"Dualism" is conceptualized within existing theories. Naturalistic dualism theory, starting with a great degree of *theoretical overlap* (as a grounded indicator), is the work of Chalmers (1996; 2017a; 2017b; 2018). Chalmers (1996; 2017b) proposed a theory of *Naturalistic Dualism*, which tends to ground and support the proposed holoplexity theory in several ways. Chalmers' work is separate from the work of many others in that it continuously identifies and actively pursues a solution to *the meta-problem of*

consciousness (see Chalmers, 2018). Chalmers' body of work is extensive and has served as an organizational model for this study.

The proposed theory was grounded in Chalmers' call for an *"extra ingredient"* (1996; 2017a; 2017b, italics added). Admittedly, this extra ingredient call was further indicated by the recognition that current theories do not fully explain consciousness, but instead rather tend to deny, reduce, or re-label consciousness—except for one esoteric quantum theory by David Bohm (1980) discovered near the end of this research. By stating the need for "a new component" to "bridge the gap" (Chalmers, 1996, p. 8) between the two concepts of *functionalism* and *experience*, the tone was set precisely for what was being sought (i.e., "explanatory gap," Levine, 1983). Chalmers further wrote that he believed, "[T]he identity involving consciousness is not derivable from physical facts" (Chalmers, 1996, p. 10). This statement indicates that Chalmers believes consciousness itself lies outside the physical—or perhaps something that underlies the physical.

At this point in the study, grounding concepts in the consciousness literature were examined, but at a specific, *most* basic level. *Grounding concepts* are concepts that are viable in their originating works as theoretical constructs. Such concepts, while remaining compatible with reality as we know it, would then tend to add plausibility and thus support the proposed holoplexity theory. However, the search is conducted at the *most basic* level at this point. Such a depth of inquiry typically leaves the realm of psychology and enters the domains of physics and philosophy.

Grounded indication: Heisenberg

Regarding the findings that led to Heisenberg's *uncertainty principle* and the term *measurement* (as it leads to *collapse*), Chalmers (1996) stated, "[I]t can seem that consciousness is the only non-arbitrary way to distinguish measurement from other physical events. If so, then consciousness may be present in quantum mechanics' very foundations" (p. 20). Here, Chalmers gives a very clear indication that he believes consciousness itself is somehow associated with quantum physics.

Also included nearer to this level of analysis is the *duality of consciousness* itself. The holoplexity theory, as proposed, states as a given that matter and energy exist as we currently know them, and this novel theory is completely compatible with classical level physics as currently understood. There is no difference on the macro-level of analysis. The integral difference is that *matter* (as we understand it) is never completely independent of the underlying *dimension of consciousness itself* because it is both: (a) ultimately comprised of consciousness, and (b) exists within the larger dimension of consciousness. Given these propositions, it is hypothesized that all forms of matter, energy, and even space have at least a *dual nature*. And that "dual nature" is an inherent connection with the larger dimension of consciousness itself. It is hypothesized that it is this *dual nature* constitutes the connection between the human *physical world* and the primary *larger dimension of consciousness itself.*

Grounded indication: McGinn

Due to its non-apparent manifestation, it is speculated that the *primary dimension of consciousness itself* fits the *hidden aspect* conclusion of McGinn (1995). The researcher interprets this because it is "hidden" outside of what humans conceive of as *time* (using common language to generate an image). Because human beings have limited conceptual knowledge that is independent of *time*, and because human language reflects this limitation, this complex concept is difficult to imagine (or to write about).

In 2011, tellingly, McGinn wrote:

> Consciousness is indeed continuous with the other forms of matter/energy, meshing with other forms, sharing their energy content, causally interacting with them—and that is an important part of the reason to suppose that there is a single reality underlying both consciousness and the rest of nature. (p. 187)
> Consciousness is indeed continuous with the other forms of matter/energy, meshing with other forms, sharing their energy content, causally interacting with them—and that is an important

part of the reason to suppose that there is a single reality underlying both consciousness and the rest of nature. (p. 187)

Here McGinn lends clear grounded support to the idea that consciousness itself tends to underlie all else in the universe.

Grounded indication: Wheeler

The proposed holoplexity theory fits the *apparent basis* of reality as conceptualized by the *bit* (Wheeler, 1989). Given the previously explained re-conceptualizations of the *bit* by Wheeler and other theorists, all theories that contain the concept of the *dual aspect* then ground and lend specific conceptual support to this proposed novel theory. Specifically, by theoretical sampling, it was found that there are four specific theorists and theories that appear to provide grounded conceptual support at this specific level of inquiry for the proposed holoplexity theory.

Grounded indication: Chalmers

David Chalmers (2017b) stated that his *suggested outline* for an eventual theory contains a kind of "innocent version of dualism" (p. 364), meaning that at the macro-level of organization, there is likely to exist a separation within consciousness itself as expressed: (1) manifestly in materialism; and (2) ontologically in consciousness itself. This is fully consistent with this theory, as well as the impetus and rationale behind the name choice—the many manifestations (-plexity) originating from one (holo-) source.

Chalmers believed that consciousness was *non-reductive* and did *not emerge* from materials. This is a *crucial* but *fine* distinction between the proposed holoplexity theory, Chalmers' theory, and the various *theories of emergence*. Within holoplexity theory, it is hypothesized that it is an integral interface that *does emerge* from the mechanisms of the brain (and *not* consciousness itself that emerges). The proposed interface is electromagnetic in expression. As mentioned, it is an interface, temporary in nature, electromagnetic in expression, and not reducible to the brain mechanisms that "handle it." It is the *interaction* between the humanly enabled interface and consciousness itself— which is then subsequently apprehended by human brain mechanisms—which constitutes human consciousness.

In other words, what humans experience as *phenomenal consciousness* is a personal human brain's apprehension of the inherent connection of the "emerged interface" to the dimension of consciousness itself. Thus, it is true that human consciousness is *not reducible* to the mechanisms that seemingly gave rise to it, however, the properties of consciousness itself do play an integral role in the humanly enabled interface emerging.

The *emergence* of the human interface is important because the concept of *emergence* remains still relevant. Although most emergence-based theories of consciousness claim that consciousness itself is (reduced to) an *emergent by-product* of brain function, the researcher believes this contention is wrong. *Consciousness itself is being confused as the human interface only in emergence-based theories.* It is the *interface* that *emerges* to connect with what already exists—the larger *consciousness itself.*

In addition to proffering his naturalistic dualism theory (Chalmers, 1996); Chalmers (2017b) provides guidelines in which *principles* are described and believed to operate as *constraints* or criteria to be met for an eventual theory envisioned as a *satisfactory* account to explain the hard problem of consciousness. The first principle is the "Principle of Structural Coherence" (p. 368) and the second is the "Principle of Organization Invariance" (p. 365).

The principle of "structural coherence" states (Chalmers, 2017b):

> It is this isomorphism between the structures of consciousness and awareness that constitutes the principle of structural coherence. This principle reflects the *central fact* that even though cognitive processes do not conceptually entail facts about conscious experience, consciousness and cognition do not float free of one another but *cohere in an intimate way.* (p. 367, italics added)

The proposed holoplexity theory fully comports with this principle and goes one step further: *awareness* and *human consciousness* are overlapping sub-concepts of the larger consciousness itself. According to the proposed theory, awareness and human consciousness are distinct, but comingled phenomena. *Awareness* is a result of the human experience of consciousness via the interface. And *human consciousness* is the phenomenal experience of the electromagnetic interface with the larger dimension of consciousness itself. (Recalling that the distinction between the larger "consciousness itself" and individual "human consciousness" appears to be sequentially separated by events and thus in time by at least .1-second.) The principle of structural coherence, as determined by Chalmers, provides theoretical support for the proposed Holoplexity theory.

The second principle, as determined by Chalmers, is that of organizational invariance. This principle states (Chalmers, 2017b):

> This principle states that any two systems with the same fine-grained functional organization will have qualitatively identical experiences. If the causal patterns of the neural organization were duplicated in silicon, for example, with a silicon chip for every neuron and the same patterns of interaction, the same experiences would arise. (p.368)

The proposed Holoplexity theory is fully grounded by this principle, with one minor (possibly negligible) distinction. Of the two hypothetical experiences, one biologically based, and the other silicon-based, the resultant experiences would be *slightly* different because they would occur from different temporal and spatial perspectives in the physical world (much like human twins' experiences in the physical world are, separated by degrees of time and space). Other than that fine distinction, there is no theoretical reason why they would not be identical in other ways. As this theory appears to be in accord with this principle, the researcher is satisfied that Chalmers' principle of organizational invariance provides grounded support for the proposed Holoplexity theory.

Grounded indication: Carruthers

The dual-content theory by *Carruthers* (2017) began as a *Higher-Order Thought* (HOT) theorist, then seemed to have realized, correctly, that there must be *more*. Carruthers realized that HOT theorists are not different from identity theorists, meaning that they equate consciousness with some *level* or *quantity* of higher-order thinking alone. However, Carruthers recognized that perceptions bring in *new* raw information not previously in the brain. The brain can then *immediately* assimilate this new data into its cognition. Carruthers must have realized the conundrum here—how can this be? Carruthers' observation and conclusion are consistent with the proposed holoplexity theory: that perceptions must have a *dual content*. Carruthers (2017) stated, "Hence the appropriateness of the label 'dual-content theory': for it is one and the same perceptual state that has both first-order and higher-order analog/non-conceptual contents" (p. 290).

This is a *key* distinction, which removes it from the category of HOT theories and into a category that does not diminish the primacy of the ontology of consciousness itself. Insightfully, referring to Bach-y-Rita and Kercel (2003), Carruthers outlines an alternatively *generated* interface. Carruthers (2017) wrote:

> The point can be illustrated concerning an example of how first-order perceptual contents can be transformed by changes in consumer systems; namely, prosthetic vision (Bach-y-Rita, 1995). Blind subjects can be fitted with a device that converts the output from a hand-held or head-mounted video camera into a pattern of electrically-induced tactile stimulation—in the original experiments, via a pad extending across the subject's back; in more recent experiments (and because of its greater sensitivity), via an attachment to the subject's tongue. Initially, of course, the subject just feels patterns of gentle tickling sensations spreading over the area in question, while the camera scans what is in front of them. But provided that they are allowed to control the movements of the camera themselves, their experiences after a time acquire three-dimensional distal intentional contents, representing the positions and movements

of objects in space. It seems that what transforms the contents of these subjects" experiences is that the tactile contents are mapped on the area of the brain that is concerned with building spatial representations (Bach-y-Rita & Kercel, 2003). By the novel use that is made of those states, they thereby acquire new contents. It is claimed by Carruthers (2000) that essentially the same mechanism is at work in the generation of dual-content perceptual states. (p. 295)

Carruthers appeared to have recognized that outside *new* information was coming in. The term *generation* suggests that something new is now present which was not previously. Carruthers seemed to have recognized that what was *generated* as a kind of "interface" may be alternatively described as a *dual-content perceptual state*. Once the interface is generated, the *unfolding* of information is thought to be *automatic and unavoidable* (given that information at this level of organization is electromagnetic in expression). Human brain mechanisms can apprehend the information from the larger consciousness itself at this point. It is here that the humanly generated interface has connected with the dimension of consciousness itself, both by virtue of the information unfolding within the brain and because the human brain exists *within* the larger consciousness itself.

Put another way, brain mechanisms connect the properties of the *dual-content perceptions* to *consciousness itself* via the interface (the hypothesized process is explained more fully in the following section). Once these smaller connections are made (the interface is established), the immediacy and continuity of consciousness itself are had. Again, this is hypothesized to be automatic and unavoidable as it is an electromagnetic exchange (at this level).

It is hypothesized in holoplexity theory that the brain mechanisms' architecture, or structural arrangement, enables and supports the unfolding of the non-spatial, non-temporal data into something useful for human 3-D understanding. (This is human learning, creating *meaning* and interpreting what percepts are coming in, somewhat akin to computer languages being formatted and therefore *compatible*.) Information coming in for a blind person would be qualitatively different from a sighted person who is deaf. The human side of the *interface* is limited in this regard as some information may go unrealized (i.e., microwaves, radio waves, etc.)

All information is hypothesized to exist in the primary dimension of consciousness itself. Once this dimension is linked to the humanly generated *interface* there is an unfolding of information and a change of informational statuses made between them (by creating one moment from the previous moment via consciousness itself). Alternatively said, *time* has passed when one constellation of information changes to a slightly different constellation of information, thereby containing two moments in time. The electromagnetic properties of immediacy and continuity of the perception via consciousness itself (post-perception: *human consciousness*) after the exchange via the interface are the proposed answer to the "explanatory gap" (Carruthers, 2017, p. 291, Chalmers, 1996; Levine, 2001). This question is answered when combined with the circular system of *self* and its ability to experience and learn. This account and electromagnetic properties may also tend to offer insight into the "binding problem," a term coined by Treisman in 1980. The "binding problem" is the question of how the background, objects, and emotional features are experienced as a single experience.

Grounded indication: Velmans

Reflexive monism theory by *Velmans* (1990; 2008; 2017a) provides a counterintuitive perspective. Another grounded indication was provided within this clarifying quote by Velmans (2017a):

> In this monist vision, there is one universe (the *thing itself*), with relatively differentiated parts in the form of conscious beings like ourselves, each with a unique, conscious view of the larger universe of which it is a part. Insofar as we are parts of the universe that, in turn, experience the larger universe, we participate in a reflexive process whereby the universe experiences itself. (p. 361)

This theoretical perspective begins with the notion that all is *one*, and that one *is consciousness*. It is a very short logical jump from there to the notion that the mechanisms of consciousness, and information they apprehend, are composed of consciousness itself (although *differentiated*). Being composed of *a single thing but differentiated* can again be easily and readily interpreted as an alternative definition of *dual-aspect*.

Within *reflexive monism* theory, what is apprehended by human senses are *not* the things themselves, but the energy having been affected by the existence of those things in such a way that they represent an aspect of—and a connection to—those things. Again, all occur within the larger dimension of consciousness itself. In the proposed holoplexity theory, it is hypothesized that what is transmitted is the consciousness aspect of a *thing/energy-interaction* which resides as a differentiated part of the consciousness itself primary dimension. The proposed holoplexity theory hypothesizes that within consciousness itself inheres all things. As such, they can be accessed because of their occupancy within the dimension of consciousness itself. It is hypothesized that the dimension itself has no spatial features and no temporal features, but contains the representations of all things (and immediate interconnections of all things by virtue of itself).

In other words, once the connection between the *object* and *observer* is made, it becomes reified within the larger dimension of consciousness itself. This is because human perception is not separate from the connection made within the larger dimension of consciousness itself. There is a kind of internal and external connection made— both simultaneously *to consciousness itself* and *of consciousness itself*.

In the human physical world (3-D + time), this connection is seen as mere perception. However, within the larger dimension of consciousness itself, this *perceptual apprehension* is as real as anything else that occupies that dimension. The *realness* of this connection is transmitted from one moment into the next moment via its connection again within the overall larger and everchanging dimension of consciousness itself. Again, it is the ever-changing nature of consciousness itself that is hypothesized to drive reality *and not time*.

As consciousness itself is conceptualized as a primary dimension, it is hypothesized that such a dimension has a continuum or a continuity, a fluidity, a boundarylessness, as well as a timelessness, of the information that occupies this dimension. What this is hypothesized to mean is that there are *no discrete pieces* of information in this dimension. The information here is whole and only *linked outwardly by change* (humanly understood as "time") however while being linked *intrinsically* by *consciousness itself.*

It is hypothesized that there is *no time* in this dimension. There is no before and after, but there *just is what is* within this singularity of potential. When an electromagnetic link is made via energy to an object, it is intrinsically linked *within* this dimension of consciousness (linked without spatial extension and without time). Thus, in the *human physical world*, what seems to be a *mere perception* is, a very *real connection* made between the object and the observer (at the level of the larger dimension of consciousness itself). Once that real connection is made in one moment, that connection is transferred to the next moment as *recorded* within the dimension of consciousness itself. This is thought to be what makes the perception *real* in the human physical world. The *percept-of-the-object* is not different from the *object-as-perceived* within this larger dimension; they are one and the same at the most basic level of consciousness itself (see Velmans, 1990).

Holoplexity theory can be conceived as a workable model for the unexplained concept of "perceptual projection" (Velmans, 2017a, p. 355) within the reflexive monism theory. Perceptual projection refers to the question of how proximal neural causes within the brain support experienced events that seem to be outside the brain. It is hypothesized that the primary dimension of consciousness itself constitutes what we perceive as reality (although .1-second removed). It is the .1-second removal that is hypothesized to constitute the "hidden dimension" aspect (McGinn, 2017) or missing "extra ingredient" aspect (Chalmers, 2017b). It is this *hidden dimension* that also tends to offer a viable solution to the mystery of perceptual projection.

In other words, holoplexity theory conceives of the dimension of consciousness itself as affecting *all*. It links the object-in-the-world *simultaneously to* the object-as-represented-in-the-mind. This is hypothesized to happen because the physical brain itself exists within the larger consciousness itself. Again, it is both an internal (within brain generated interface) and external (brain within larger consciousness itself) change. Recall that the brain and its products occupy the dimension of consciousness itself, while simultaneously taking in information about the world around it.

Perception remains perception as we know it; what is different is the ontological status of perception. Perception is conceived of within the proposed holoplexity theory as a *more real* connection within human consciousness than previously attributed. That (*more direct* than previously attributed) connection is hypothesized transferred from one moment to the next moment by the everchanging nature of *consciousness itself* which interacts with *all* in the human physical world. This everchanging interaction was previously confused as the fourth dimension of time. However, time seems to be more accurately described as being a secondary effect, a byproduct, or a result of, this everchanging interaction.

The researcher maintains the hypothesis that the *connection between all things* remains "hidden" (McGinn, 1995) between one moment and the next moment but as *recorded* or reified within the dimension of consciousness itself (with no spatial or temporal features). Consequently, perception is as real as anything else because of its *connection* within this dimension.

This concludes the theories researched that tend to illustrate the *duality of matter*. This duality is conceived to be one-half of the proposed *interface*. The other half of the proposed *interface* is the *duality of consciousness itself*. This needs to be stated explicitly because it is perhaps *the* core sub-category of the proposed holoplexity theory. It is the *key* mechanism by which *the dimension of consciousness itself* interfaces with *the physical world of human beings*. And, once the individual *human interface* is connected to the *dimension of consciousness* the information from it becomes *a personal experience* as a result of it being apprehended by (and thus becoming the possession of) human brain mechanisms.

Theme 4:
The Neurocognitive COS as
the Embodied "Experiencer" of the Interface

Recalling that the neurocognitive COS is not synonymous with the embodied "I," it is hypothesized that the *neurocognitive self-referential awareness* (COS) being assembled and installed creates "the mind" as we know it. The mind then acts as an interface that is subsequently connected to the dimension of consciousness itself through the apprehension of information from that source. This apprehension creates a two-part electromagnetic interface with the dimension of consciousness itself because (1) it is established via neurocognitive mechanisms of the human brain, and (2) the brain is proposed to exist within the dimension of consciousness itself (along with the rest of the world). Although the neurocognitive parts are biological, their expression is *electromagnetic* (i.e., the *mind* as opposed to the *brain*). Once this interface is achieved, the immediacy and continuity of the dimension of consciousness itself take primacy. It is believed that the nature of the link is automatic, instantaneous, and seamless in its integration.

"Concept of Self" Theorists

The researcher hypothesizes the existence of a *temporary* sentience acquisition system (TSAS). Sentience is expressed here as the *onset* and *ongoing experience* of "self-awareness," which is defined as self-referential conscious awareness. The exact brain mechanisms that comprise the TSAS are not the specific focus of this hypothesized construct, but very likely include the temporary cross-wiring of infant brains, infant internal body maps, infant eidetic memory, the mirror neuron system, and the events of infant neural pruning or apoptosis. As several of the mechanisms that comprise the TSAS appear only temporarily in infant neurodevelopment, the TSAS likely exists for the *sole purpose of achieving sentience* before the onset of apoptosis.

Sentience itself, as a concept of knowledge, must then be combined with ongoing consciousness—and *into* ongoing consciousness—to generate the stable neurocognitive concept of *self* (COS). The COS combines the intellectual knowledge of "self-awareness" with "bodily awareness." With ongoing experience and additional social knowledge, the *theory of mind* develops. In infancy, it is the amygdala (as the hippocampus is immature at this time) that aggregates these neurocognitive concepts together with sensory stimuli. As a result, it is proposed that the COS has a *deeply personal feel* attached to it (Carter, 2010). It is this *feeling* that may address the *explanatory gap* (Levine, 1983). Importantly, note that here again the *phenomenological "I"* is synonymous with the *neurocognitive COS* (as well as the *embodied "I"*).

Once developed, the COS is thought to necessarily become encoded into *all* memories created to be effective. The COS is further hypothesized to be encoded into all subsequent incoming sensory streams and products by virtue of the hippocampi and amygdalae. The hippocampus is where memories are consolidated, and it is proposed that this is the point at which the COS is *encoded into* the sensory streams and products. Being *encoded into all memories* created is synonymous with becoming an element of all memories. Memories are then believed to become retrievable by their constituent elements (Carter, 2010).

As the COS is encoded into each memory and it becomes retrievable by the COS, it is hypothesized to become the *primary method of retrieval*. Thus, the COS becomes the *central organizing mechanism* (COM) of the brain. The COM is then hypothesized to tie together memories across time and additionally integrate them with the here-and-now.

Alternatively said, this core category is a unique aspect of the overall theory because it hypothesized that the COS, once established, is encoded into *all* interceptive and exteroceptive stimuli. How and why this is important is once the COS is encoded into these stimuli, elements are thought to be retrievable by virtue of this *code*. It is this code that then becomes a central organizing mechanism (COM) of the *brain* and the *self*.

This method of memory retrieval is well-established in the literature (retrieval by virtue of an element of a memory). How this common method of memory retrieval works is, again, not the focus here. Rather the focus is that the relatively unique idea that it is an *idea*, or a concept, that defines the *self*. This notion of self as a mere idea is not new to consciousness theorizing but is made explicit here, and further explicated as a *neurocognitive code*. Noting that we have now moved from the *brain* (biological/physical) to the *mind* (ideological/electromagnetic). The brain deals with specific neurobiological parts, whereas the mind deals with ideas and concepts. This is a key distinction being made explicit here. The TSAS is a *brain* mechanism, but its product COS is of the *mind*. The COS being utilized as a tool within the mind (to organize other mind-products) makes it a *mechanism* of the mind. This distinction between brain and mind *is* an integral part of understanding how the brain creates the mind, and in turn, how it is the mind that interacts with consciousness itself. They are thought to be compatible with electromagnetic entities.

As this specific part of the holoplexity theory overlaps "the easy problems of consciousness" with "the hard problem of consciousness," there is a great deal of conceptual support that is grounded in the literature. Some aspect of the COS as "experiencer" is similarly indicated as *reflexivity* by Seager and Bourget (2017), as *a mind-reading faculty* by Carruthers (2017, p. 294), as *the dynamic core* by Edelman and Tononi (2000), as *a vehicular property* by Kriegel (2002), as *a core consciousness* by Damasio (1999), as (one of) *the brain's three minds* by Klemm (2014), again as *the dynamic core* by Tononi (2004), and as *reflexive* by Velmans (1990).

Theme 5:
Overlapping Brain Systems and Structures Create
Conditions for Consciousness Architecture to Unfold

Neurocognitive theorists

It is hypothesized that reality as humanly experienced (aka *phenomenal*) is expressed between specific structures of the human brain (that are in turn contained within the dimension of consciousness itself). The specific structures that are commonly known as 3-D are composed of the (sub-) dimensions of length, width, and height. These structures themselves are hypothesized to exist *within* consciousness itself and *unfold* from consciousness itself. It is proposed that the juxtaposition of the brain structures (architecture) allows these structures to *unfold*, similarly as 3-D information comes from juxtaposed 2-D information.

The redundant sensory systems of vision, olfaction, and audition are examples of *redundant and overlapping systems* that create an emergent property that is not found in either of the individual systems that were combined to create it (Carter, 2010; 2014). This is a key construct of the proposed theory. The underlying brain mechanisms of this analogy were extrapolated to create an understanding of the experience of phenomenal 4-D reality. Ironically, this is the level at which the concept of multiple drafts by Dennett (1991) may have some footing as a mechanism, while it still does not explain human consciousness and still denies consciousness itself.

Further, the phenomena of *blindsight, blindsmell, blindtouch, reflex operations, the reticular activating system, REM sleep, the fight-flight response,* and *the Libet experiment* (1985) together *all* tend to indicate to the researcher the existence of still-operational ancient sensory systems (Carter, 2010; Klemm, 2014). These ancient systems are hypothesized to operate *in conjunction with* the modern human sensory systems of today. It is proposed that these overlapping systems are separated, not only by position (space), but also by disparate function, and staggered in sequence or in time. Generalizing from these concepts, this spatial and temporal separation between systems gives rise to the emergent property of a dynamic, phenomenal 4-D consciousness. A property not found in any of the underlying but overlapping systems.

The more ancient systems get stimuli to *awareness* in approximately .1-second (Blackmore, 2004; Carter, Aldridge, Page & Parker, 2014). The modern human sensory system gets stimuli to *awareness* in approximately .5-seconds (Blackmore, 2004; Carter, Aldridge, Page & Parker, 2014). It is hypothesized that human consciousness, in its evolving 4-D form, exists in and emerges from— within this continuing, dynamic .4-second timeframe overlap. The "brain's three minds" (Klemm, 2013) essentially pass the thought around between them, changing it; comprehending it; then immediately changing it again.

Abductive analysis narrative regarding
"unfolding" of consciousness

Does primary consciousness inherently contain structure? Or is this structure imposed upon it by the limitations of human perceptual and interpretative systems? Upon contemplation of these questions of consciousness, what appeared most striking was the notion that consciousness seemed to qualify as a kind of *pure potentiality*. Often, when the researcher needed a *theoretical substitute for a concept* while theorizing; the notion of *pure potentiality* as a concept that seemed synonymous with consciousness itself would work excellently. It still does today. Given this informal stand-in heuristic, it is *more likely* that the limitations of the human perceptual and interpretative systems impose their limitations on our connection to consciousness itself than that to think that consciousness itself is limited in *any* manner.

The hypothetical architecture as contained within consciousness itself is speculative but does have conceptual support in the literature. It is also somewhat intuitive once a bit of thought is spent on the idea. Again, the contrasting but overlapping information of two separate 2-D perceptual informational streams appears to *unfold* into phenomenal 3-D dimensionality. Depth perception is a "real ability" and not an inference of 3-D (Carter, 2009). From this factual *system,* the structure of 3-D must be pre-existent within the information itself. This aspect of vision as it relates to the *unfolding of 3-D information* is well established in the wealth of literature specific to the visual system. This concept will be expanded upon later to include what can be thought of as a phenomenal 4-D in time.

It is further hypothesized that additional information may be *unfolded* when different streams of information are contrasted and combined while overlapping (aka *integration*). It is further proposed that upon this sensory information being unfolded and combined (integrated), it becomes apprehended by brain mechanisms. This is when two things occur *simultaneously*: (1) the act of "apprehension" is synonymous with *perception* in the physical world, and (2) this concurrently constitutes a connection in the dimension of consciousness itself (as the brain exists within the larger dimension of consciousness itself). This concurrent connectivity of (a) the brain to mind; (b) mind to consciousness itself; and (c) the brain within consciousness itself is hypothesized to occur as an electromagnetic function of the duality of matter and the duality of consciousness.

Grounded indications of "unfolding" within existing theories

Tononi (2017a) provides supporting evidence here within his information integration theory. Tononi's writing is highly complex and technical, but as far as it is understood, the researcher pieces together what are believed to be similar, but not exactly parallel, constructs between the two theories, expressed in different languages. Regarding the *physical mechanisms of the brain*, Tononi (2017a) states, "We also have good, abundant evidence that a particular portion of the world—a set of neural units within the brain—constitutes the *physical substrate* of individual consciousness (PSC)" (p. 244). Further stating specifically:

> Hence the PSC must specify a cause-effect structure that is not generic, but has a specific form—a specific composition of specific cause-effect repertoires, bound together in various ways—and thereby differing in its specific way from other possible ones. Information is another requirement for existence, as something can only exist in a specific way, and not generically" (p. 245).

Additionally, it was stated by Tononi, "Together, the cause-effect repertoires specified by each composition of elements within a system compose a specific *cause-effect structure*" (p. 245, italics and bold added).

Tononi, a medical doctor, seems to be coming at the problem from the inside-out; in a more systematic, technical fashion, while the researcher comes at the same problem from the outside in—in a more holistic, phenomenal fashion. Each theory is describing the same phenomenon. That phenomenon is that there are brain architectures that match our phenomenal experiences.

However, this is where the proposed theory parts from Tononi's theory. While it is true that the holoplexity theory postulates a kind of *integration of information* similar to the information integration theory, exactly how the integration is proposed to occur is explicitly different. The holoplexity theory states that once the interface is erected and assembled, it can extract non-apparent information from existing information. How so? The answer is that this information is hypothesized to be expressed within this dynamic electromagnetic system of *unfolding* or *integration*. This hypothesis was surmised from the observation that two streams of similar information can produce information not evident in either single stream when juxtaposed electromagnetically (2-D to 3-D). It was then further hypothesized that this can occur at an *electromagnetic level* as with other kinds of information.

There is nothing magical or mystical about this process. It is a kind of *unfolding* of a rich blend of information (or *integration* in the language of Tononi (2017)) that is the content of our phenomenal consciousness. The hypothesized electromagnetic connection created is believed to be a real thing—a real thing that exists both at the level of mind and within primary consciousness itself. This hypothetical *connection* is made when the dimension (sideways to the *flow* time) of consciousness itself—interacts with—both *the-thing-perceived* (in the world) and the *percept-of-the-thing* (in the mind) **simultaneously**.

Velmans (2017a), within his *reflexive monism theory,* pointed out a missing piece of that theory that the concept(s) of *unfolding* or *integration* of consciousness itself may explain nicely. The missing piece is "perceptual projection" (Velmans, 2017a, p. 355). Velmans elaborates, "nothing physical, observable from a third-person perspective, is projected from the brain…Even though the proximal neural causes and correlates of neural causes and correlates of conscious experiences are inside our brains, our experienced phenomenal bodies and worlds appear to be outside our brains." Read slowly and carefully, the reader may appreciate that the application of the processes of *unfolding* or *integration* to both (1) consciousness itself and (2) the brain-within-consciousness itself—simultaneously— is proposed to answer this *missing piece* of "perceptual projection."

In other words, it is hypothesized that it is (a) consciousness itself as subdivided and acting as (b) "the-thing-itself" and (c) "the-precept-of-the-thing" *both* further interact within the (d) dimension of consciousness itself to create this complex phenomenon of *perceptual projection*. One can see why this such an interaction may be referred to as either an *unfolding* as in holoplexity theory or alternatively an *integrating* as in information integration theory—depending upon the conceptual perspective.

Summary of Advanced Coding

Consciousness itself (as primary and fundamental) is hypothesized to predate the universe. Consciousness itself is also hypothesized to comprise the underlying structure of reality at one level, in addition to being thought to comprise all matter and energy at a different level. Consciousness is hypothesized to be *the causal factor* of time. Human senses are hypothesized to be developed to capture the electromagnetic manifestation(s) of consciousness itself. As consciousness itself (as a dimension) is hypothesized to be positioned as a precursor to the flow of time, it is effectively hidden. Consciousness itself is also thought to exist in *all things* as manifested (matter/electromagnetism) including other-than-manifest (non-spatial, non-temporal), and as the structural architecture of reality (physical 3-D and phenomenal 4-D). As such, consciousness itself is hypothesized to be both an external and internal participant when sensory perceptions (as electromagnetic energy) become neurocognitive information (as electromagnetic energy). Never is consciousness itself hypothesized to be separate from *any* activity or thing.

Consciousness itself is proposed to be *unfolded within* overlapping brain structures thereby creating the "architecture of reality" hypothesized to be inherent within consciousness itself. As all of this is hypothesized to be electromagnetic in expression and its manifestation, *there is no binding problem*. This proposed holoplexity theory is then proposed to have closed the "explanatory gap" (Levine, 1983). The holoplexity theory offered a coherent conceptualization as to "how information becomes experience" (Chalmers, 2017a) because as consciousness itself (as information) becomes apprehended within the human brain (becoming *human consciousness*), the electromagnetic manifestations become apprehended by, and interpreted, by the concept of self (COS). The COS is the phenomenal "I." Being *"apprehended by"* and *"interpreted by"* the phenomenal "I" is the definition of having become its *"possession."* If true, this would account for the phenomenal mistaken dichotomy of the mind-body problem. Once *possessed* by the COS (phenomenal "I"), this way of thinking becomes the COM (central organizing mechanism) of the brain and the mind.

Conclusion

This process contained three (3) levels of analysis. This analytical strategy is an attempt to reconnect the evolving analysis back to the original research question and to demonstrate research transparency within the grounded theory methodology via a storyline technique. This is a reconceptualization of consciousness (as both *human consciousness—and—consciousness itself*) which is firmly grounded within the existing information (theory) in the field (theoretical literature at the time of this writing). This reconceptualization amounts to an original and newly proposed theory for several reasons. Holoplexity theory holds *consciousness itself* to be ontologically preexistent, while hypothesizing that *human consciousness* is emergent from (but not reducible to) the confluences of brain structures, electromagnetic properties, and the dual properties of sensory information (consciousness itself). Holoplexity theory as a reconceptualization makes a *basic distinction* between primary *consciousness itself* (as fundamental consciousness) and *human consciousness* ("consciousness itself" as apprehended within the human brain by "our idea of ourselves").

Conclusions,
Recommendations and Limitations

Presented in this chapter are concluding statements and recommendations. Conclusions are not the same as findings, nor are they interpretations. Rather, conclusions are assertions based upon the findings. Conclusions are then based upon findings and arguably warranted by those findings.

Recommendations are the applications of those same conclusions (Bloomberg & Volpe, 2018). Limitations identify the restrictions and weaknesses inherent in the study. Limitations include considerations about the scope of the study.

Conclusions

I believe I have generated an original, empirically compatible, non-reductive theory of consciousness that offers a viable answer to the hard problem of consciousness. I define "viability" as the ability to work successfully in the long term.

This concluding statement is based upon findings but is not a reiteration of findings or an interpretation of the same findings. I assert that Holoplexity theory does answer that hard problem of consciousness. In reviewing the theory and reviewing the process, Holoplexity theory fits the definition of an original work.

However, Holoplexity theory can also be seen as a series of logically coherent sub-theories that have explanatory power regarding the hard problem of consciousness. Not every one of the sub-theories is original in their inception here. Not every one of the sub-theories is equally as "theoretically strong."

The hard problem of consciousness has endured unanswered for so long because it is a truly difficult problem. I assert that the difficulty in the problem lies in underlying presumptions contained within the language used to convey the problem itself (the hard problem of consciousness) and in the various approaches to the sub-problems that arise in pursuit of an answer.

In my opinion, likely the most important aspect of Holoplexity theory is also perhaps its most conceptually supported or theoretically grounded—I am referring to "panpsychism." Just within this study, *panpsychism* seemed to be emerging as a viable conceptual solution to aspects of the questions of *consciousness itself*, as was seen more directly in the works of Strawson (physicalist panpsychism theory), Chalmers (naturalistic dualism theory), Velmans (reflexive monism theory), Carruthers (dual-content theory), Bohm (implicate order theory), and Maturana and Varela (the Santiago theory of cognition)—and more *indirectly* as seen in the works of Zeki (microconsciousness theory), the quantum theorists (Hameroff and Penrose, Eccles, McGinn, Atmanspacher, and Bohm), and the HOA theorists (Rosenthal, and others).

This is not to mention the many books related to the concept of panpsychism that are not included here. Panpsychism is a counterintuitive concept; but after a bit of thought, it becomes more palatable. For me, after this study, I am convinced of it.

Recalling that theory does not prove a theory, my goal is not to "prove" anything, but only to generate a viable theory. It is my opinion that this specific aspect of the theory is viable.

If we take panpsychism as true, then that necessarily means a separation, at least in expression, between "human consciousness" and "consciousness itself." It is my opinion that this is part of why there is so much confusion in the literature regarding the term "consciousness." And further, it is part of why the hard problem of consciousness has endured for so long.

Whether or not "consciousness itself" underlies the other three dimensions and is the causal factor of time may seem tangential to the question of how consciousness leads to experience. Except that it appears not to be tangential, but instead integral to that question. The term "experience" is a loaded word. First, it implies a human phenomenon or at least the phenomenon of a consciously aware being. Secondly, time is inherent in such a word. Because of these things, the questions about "consciousness itself" being the primary dimension (in the strongest sense of the word) and its relationship to time is relevant.

The Santiago theory of cognition (Maturana & Varela, 1980) does an excellent job of explaining this phenomenon in general terms. But first, let us examine the efficacy of the claim that "consciousness itself" drives time. Admittedly, this is a lonelier proposition, because I have found only the physicist Hameroff (2003) who explicitly states this. I am sure other researchers have concluded this in other contexts, but I have necessarily excluded them to maintain the scope of this inquiry. Yet, this means that this concept has a measure of conceptual support that is grounded in the consciousness literature. If the perceived isomorphism between "consciousness itself" and "quantum mechanics" is taken as true, then there is a great deal of suggestion that consciousness itself has an intimate relationship to time.

The Santiago theory of cognition makes a claim of autopoiesis, which is a self-creating system. This eloquently explains how "human consciousness" may arise from human neuronal complexity but is silent on how simple consciousness first enters the picture. Recall that getting "consciousness" from non-consciousness is akin to magic and an unacceptable departure from logic. However, if the notion of panpsychism is adopted, then one can see the logic behind the concept of autopoiesis as it relates to "human consciousness" more clearly.

However, the Santiago theory of cognition has an even greater use. The Santiago theory uses "cognition" as a broad term to denote any "system" that "undergoes continual structural changes while preserving its weblike pattern of organization" in which the "components of the network continually produce and transform one another" (Capra & Luisi, 2019, p. 255). As such, "cognition" is likened to a "change" or a "bringing forth" in the world—and not only specific to conscious beings necessarily.

This broader term of "cognition" is useful in this theory on a more basic level of reality. Recall that my definition of time is predicated upon "change" as a concept. This overlap of concepts indicates "consciousness itself" as a concurrent idea here. My point is that the Santiago theory of cognition provides insight into an understanding of how the world, as a system, moves from one moment to the next.

Moving on, if we take the notion of "panpsychism" as true, then "human consciousness" and "consciousness itself" as separate (but related) concepts is acceptable. Holoplexity theory provided "consciousness itself" as a purveyor of change (thus, a driver of time) at a basic level of reality. This was hypothetically traced back to the first change from *nothing* to *something*, or from 0 to 1, otherwise known as the Big Bang.

As a delimitation, it is significant that Holoplexity theory is silent as to "why" this would happen (the Big Bang), or why "consciousness itself" may be conceptualized as "pure potentiality" (by the researcher) or alternatively, but similarly, conceptualized by Bohm (1980) as *continuous movement without substance* ("holomovement") and the Wheeler (2000) concept of "quantum foam."

If one can believe that "consciousness itself" underlies change. And that it is this "change" that drives our human conception of "time," then we have the basic underlying (and most counterintuitive) concepts to understanding "how information becomes experience."

The most difficult of which to conceive, and most speculative, aspect of Holoplexity theory is next. This concept is that dimensional "consciousness itself" is omnipresent, yet timeless and featureless. However, this concept is not without supporting indications. The first is logic. If "consciousness itself" is a direct precursor to time, and time is everywhere in human experience, then "consciousness itself" must be everywhere. The second is that if "consciousness itself" is the precursor to time by causing change, then it must itself be timeless. Thirdly, that "consciousness itself" is featureless or has no spatial extension is derived from "human consciousness." "Human consciousness" is defined here as "consciousness itself" as apprehended and turned in onto itself (aka reflexive) as seen in the COS. It is believed that consciousness itself is likely synonymous with quantum foam (Wheeler, 2000) or holomovement (Bohm, 1980) or as herein conceptualized by me as "pure potentiality"—which I necessarily partially define as having no temporal or spatial features (until actualized into something).

Now, moving on, it seems relatively self-evident that "consciousness itself" is never separate from anything that inheres within it or arises from it (synonymous concepts here, depending on perspective), given the concept of panpsychism. If time is defined by change, and change continuously occurs, then the dimension of "consciousness itself" must be concurrently right here, right now...and everywhere, all the time. This concept is made reified or made real, in the next step in the process of *how information becomes experience.*

First, an abstract concept must be made apparent. The mind, as an electromagnetic expression of information (which is, in turn, an expression of "consciousness itself") can be thought of as a manifestation of consciousness itself. Secondly, that "the mind" exists within the larger dimension of "consciousness itself." This is an important observation because it is believed that "the mind" has an immediate, natural connection with the larger dimension of "consciousness itself." Another way of thinking about this is that it is believed that "the mind" utilizes aspects of "consciousness itself" as its medium.

This medium, upon being electromagnetically expressed and upon being apprehended by "the mind" only then does it become "human phenomenal experience." Thus, it is never the human brain that creates "human consciousness." But the human brain uses the "reflexive property" of "consciousness itself" to identify an instance of itself. This "instance of itself" becomes a possession of the human brain as its COS (concept of self).

Recommendations

On a broad conceptual level, this study has generated an original, empirically compatible, and nonreductive theory of consciousness that offers a viable answer to the hard problem of consciousness. This is a purely theoretical study. It is a new theory generated from existing theory. Theory does not prove theory, however.

Recommendations are the *applications of* the conclusions of the study. This study has generated possible solutions to several other *hard sub-problems of consciousness* that are associated with the larger "hard problem of consciousness." Although not *proof,* if the application of Holoplexity theory can tend to address these hard sub-problems, then an indication would be given as to the explanatory power of Holoplexity theory.

The "hard sub-problems of consciousness" that became apparent during this study include: (1) the "hidden aspect or principle of space" (McGinn, 1995); (2) the mystery of "perceptual projection" (Velmans, 1990); (3) the missing "extra ingredient" (Chalmers, 1996), (4) a needed "new explanatory bridging principle" (Carter, 2002), (5) the "explanatory gap" (Levine, 1983), and (6) the "binding problem" (Treisman, 1980). The concepts of Holoplexity theory will be applied to these 6-hard sub-problems of consciousness. The explanatory power of the Holoplexity theory should become apparent or non-apparent by this demonstration.

Application 1:
The Hidden Aspect or Principle of Space

This is an interesting hard sub-problem that was not completely realized until the Holoplexity theory was completed. As I was writing this section of the study, I re-read the quote by McGinn (1995). I had not realized that McGinn predicted what I hypothesized had to exist for this theory to work. Specifically, the "non-spatial" as contained within the "spatial" within space. Let me reiterate the exact quote (McGinn, 1995) here:

> I am now in a position to state the main thesis of this paper: in order to solve the mind-body problem we need, at a minimum, a new conception of space. We need a conceptual breakthrough in the way we think about the medium in which material objects exist, and hence our conception of material objects themselves. That is the region in which our ignorance is focused: not in the details of neurophysiological activity but, more fundamentally, in how space is structured and constituted. That which we refer to when we use the word 'space' has a nature that is quite different from how we standardly conceive it to be; so different indeed, ***that it is capable of 'containing' the non-spatial*** (as we now conceive it) ***phenomenon of consciousness.*** Things in space can generate consciousness only because those things are

not, at some level, just how we conceive them to be; they harbour some hidden aspect or principle. (p. 6, italics and bold added for clarity)

McGinn's *hidden aspect or principle* is found within this theory. McGinn's prediction is found most clearly in the notion that consciousness itself underlies the other three common dimensions (3-D). What is even more powerful is that McGinn specifically states what was only implied in Holoplexity theory—that the non-spatial is "contained" within space.

In Holoplexity theory this *principle* was indicated by the "immediate connection" predicted to exist between the "dimension of consciousness itself" and the "consciousness itself" contained within "the mind" as an interface.

Coincidentally, this *hidden aspect or principle* also appears to be an overlapping concept with the "pure potentiality" conception of the researcher, the "holomovement" of Bohm (1980), and "quantum foam" of Wheeler (2000). McGinn cites our "ignorance" of "how space is structured and constituted" and further states "things in space can generate consciousness" indicating a parallel with concepts indicated by the researcher, Bohm, and Wheeler.

Application 2:
The Mystery of Perceptual Projection

The mystery of *perceptual projection* is a question of "where" a phenomenal object is located. According to Velmans (2017a), the phenomenal object seems to be out there in the world, but the neural causes and correlates of the phenomenal object are in the brain. Given this, how can we account for this apparent, "perceptual projection"? (p. 355) Said another way, Velmans (1999) states:

This reflexive model accepts conventional wisdom about the physical and neurophysiological causes of perception—for example, that there is a physical stimulus in the room that our experiences of it *represent*. But it gives a different account of the nature of the resulting experience. According to this nondualist view, when S attends to the light in a room she does not have an experience of a light "in her head or brain," with its attendant problems for science. She just sees a light in a room. (p. 301)

Holoplexity theory is completely in accord with the reflexive model of Velmans. This has a very close association with the above application (Application 1). Recall that in Holoplexity theory it is proposed that the underlying, primary, non-spatial, non-temporal dimension of "consciousness itself" is (a) "concurrently right here, right now...and everywhere and all the time" (see Concluding Statement, p. 149), and (b) that "immediate connection" was predicted to exist between the "dimension of consciousness itself" and the "consciousness itself" contained within "the mind" as an interface (see above, Application 1). This explains the "different account of the nature of the resulting experience." Why? How? Because the reflexive nature of "consciousness itself" (as the embodied "I" or neurocognitive COS) occupies the same dimension as the "light in the room" and therefore has a first-person experience and thus records the *experience* as such.

Application 3:
The Missing Extra Ingredient

Boiled down, I believe that the missing "extra ingredient" is two related missing *extra ingredients* that are integral to what makes Holoplexity theory work. I believe the first missing *extra ingredient* was the underlying dimensional nature of consciousness itself as the *primary* dimension (in the strongest sense of the word) underlying and containing all else. I think the second missing *extra ingredient* was the relationship of "the mind" to the underlying, primary dimension of "consciousness itself."

Remembering, of course, that Holoplexity theory starts with the presumption that matter arises from consciousness itself and not vice versa. The primary dimension of consciousness itself is also thought to be non-spatial and non-temporal. Further, consciousness itself is thought to be *concurrently right here, right now—and everywhere, all the time.* Difficult to conceive of when you consider it is supposed to be non-spatial and non-temporal. However, if one can get past this mind-bending concept, then one can see the efficacy of what is being said.

If this first part works, then the second missing "extra ingredient" is a natural sequitur. The mind is an electromagnetic entity. We know that consciousness itself can be expressed in this way also. Given the apparent reflexive properties of consciousness itself, it is not difficult to imagine it being a medium of sorts. When expressed electromagnetically and apprehended in its electromagnetic form, it has the rich phenomenal characteristics that we experience as human beings.

Application 4:
A Needed New Explanatory Bridging Principle

In a 2002 book entitled, *Exploring Consciousness*, Carter proposed the need for a "new explanatory bridging principle" (p.68-69). What Carter was specifically referring to was the problem of "epiphenomenalism" or the idea that human phenomenal experience is a mere aftereffect or byproduct of the brain and does not "do anything" or "control anything." Carter was saying that science has a pretty good idea of how the brain itself works, how the mind is developed, etc., but we still do not know (in 2002) how the brain/mind can affect itself.

Re-worked from the bottom-up, the Holoplexity theory explains how this happens. First, we begin with the notion that "the self" or the COS in Holoplexity theory exists. But what "the self" actually "is" differs in Holoplexity theory from what is traditionally seen. "The self" in Holoplexity theory is "consciousness itself" captured and turned back into itself, via brain mechanisms, using the apparent reflexive property it possesses. Once the idea of *itself* is established, it becomes the COS, which becomes a possession of the mind and the brain itself. The novel idea of the TSAS (temporary sentience acquisition system) is developmentally relevant here also.

This novel idea, and the related idea that "the mind" acts as an interface with the larger primary dimension of "consciousness itself," combined with traditional neuroscientific renditions of the mind (specifically the electromagnetically-based theories) account sufficiently for the causal relationship between "the mind" and "the brain." The key idea is that neurocognitive representations within the brain *are* what they appear to be.

Klemm (2014, 2019) gives the clearest explanations of the relationship between "the mind" and "the brain" that I have seen. This distinction is the point at which my theorizing about consciousness began. Klemm's (2014, 2019) descriptions are largely parallel with the researcher's concept of self (COS) alternatively and generally conceptualized as a "code." However, I also specifically add that the COS is actively being encoded into incoming stimuli streams and all other products of the mind, thereby creating the self's central organizing mechanism (COM). I also specifically state the TSAS is a specific neurodevelopmental mechanism that exists for the sole purpose of achieving sentience.

Physicist/researcher Bohm (1980) also explained a related phenomenon on the quantum level. He explained that an electron has two aspects, the field aspect, and the particle aspect. The field aspect contains "active information" which guides the behavior of the particle aspect (Pylkkanen, 2006). In a phenomenon called "back action" (Sarfatti, 1997), it is thought the particle *can reciprocally affect its field*. This is also a key concept that likely plays a role in the quantum effects of the mind/consciousness itself interaction.

This is also the demarcation point at which "the hard problem of consciousness" tends to segue into "the easy problems of consciousness." Recalling the definition of "the easy problems of consciousness" have nothing to do with intellectual difficulty or ease, but rather those problems that tend to readily lend themselves to existing methods of scientific inquiry.

Application 5:
The Explanatory Gap

In 1983, regarding the "explanatory gap," Levine wrote, "This idea is this...there is nothing we can determine about C-fiber firing that explains why having one's C-fibers fire has the qualitative character that it does..." (p. 359). In this quote, pain is equal to the firing of C-fibers.

This "hard sub-problem of consciousness" is a difficult mix of both "the easy problems" and "the hard problem"—it straddles the line. But I think I see the *spirit* of the question, with some interpretation. The question is *not* about whether pain exists, because it does (on the level of human experience). The question is also *not* about whether C-fibers (or any fiber) transmit this pain to the brain because the brain has been implicated as the location of the actualization of pain (on the level of human experience).

Levine (1983) further clarified the question, "...or, to put it another way, if what it's particularly like to have one's C-fibers fire is not explained, or made intelligible, by understanding the physical or functional properties of C-fiber firings..." (p. 359).

Strictly speaking then, the "explanatory gap" issue as brought by Levine in 1983 is an "easy problem of consciousness" (Chalmers, 2017a) question. "Easy problems" questions are outside the scope of this study. However, I believe the underlying question is not *why* the phenomenal result is as it is—but rather *how* it is that we "feel" it so intimately.

Holoplexity theory does have *something* to say about this (as reinterpreted) at the level of human experience. To begin, let me use an analogy about the color "red." Holoplexity theory says nothing about *why* the color red is experienced as phenomenally red. Holoplexity theory holds that external stimuli are "unfolded" by "the mind" over brain structures. This *unfolding* is an electromagnetic expression of information. *Why* the brain interprets the specific electromagnetic expression of information correlated to the color "red" is unknown. *That* it does is clear and self-defining. *How* it does is an "easy problem" (see "cones" in the retina and "the duplex theory of vision" as examples)—and again outside the scope of this study.

Levine in 1983 identified the "explanatory gap" issue specifically concerning the phenomenon of *pain*. Levine's issue was between the phenomenon of pain (as the feeling of pain) and its functional explanation by the idea of a C-fiber (see Kripke, 1972, 1977). Chalmers co-opted and generalized the issue to connote all experiential phenomena, as a conceptual heuristic.

Pain is an interesting point of distinction. In Holoplexity theory, we can begin with the understanding that matter arises from "consciousness itself" and not vice versa. Also, that phenomenology may be thought of as "consciousness itself" *experiencing* aspects of itself electromagnetically. We must not fall into the trap of thinking that the human body is somehow outside the entire physical realm and that all these things somehow happen outside our physical body—they may occur outside the body, but they are the same kinds of interactions that comprise our bodies.

In Holoplexity theory, the distinction was made between "interoceptive" and "exteroceptive" stimuli. *Interoceptive* and *exteroceptive* are only labels for the origins of these stimuli, relative to a human body—but *stimuli are stimuli*—period. Holoplexity theory proposes that both kinds of stimuli are further encoded or embedded with the COS, immediately upon entering the brain. This results in each kind of "experience" being **experienced as not separate** from the stimulus itself. This tends to account for the experience of *intimacy* (defined here as not separate from the self).

Remembering also that Holoplexity theory proposes each moment is immediately made available to consciousness itself as a dimension as a change. Recall that it is proposed the dimension of consciousness itself is in a constant state of flux in pure potentiality, or holomovement, or foaming (quantum). Recall that the only thing that distinguishes one moment from the next is a modicum or measure of change. Thus each "change" is immediately "recorded" in the dimension of consciousness itself and brought into the next moment. So, the intimate feeling of pain is *made real and reified* in the larger dimension. (Note: the word "immediately" is used to denote an *absence* of time here, not a short time, because again there are no temporal or spatial features in the dimension of "consciousness itself".)

Therefore, *why* the color "red" is phenomenally experienced as "red" is an "easy problem" that is outside the scope of this study (see "cones" of the retina, "duplex theory of vision," "trichromatic theory," etc.). Likewise, *why* pain is phenomenally experienced as pain is an "easy problem" and outside the scope of this study. Both questions ("red" and "pain") have to do with the mechanisms of the brain and fall under "the easy problems of consciousness" as described by Chalmers (2047a) as his first example, "the ability to discriminate, categorize, and react to environmental stimuli" (p. 32). As emotional pain has similar features to physical pain, I would hypothesize that there is a general system that reacts to unpleasant/dangerous stimuli that are wired into the brain. It is up to the brain to "discriminate the stimulus" from other stimuli, "categorize the stimulus" as unpleasant, and the pain itself may be the body's automatic "reaction to the stimulus." Thus, it is likely that the brain is itself generating the feeling of pain as a secondary reaction to its interpretation of certain kinds of stimuli.

Thus, the *why* of "pain" is an easy problem, but the *how* demarcates a boundary of "the hard problem of consciousness."

Application 6:
The Binding Problem

"The binding problem" is the question of how the background, objects, and emotional features are experienced as a single experience. "The binding problem" was situated immediately after "the explanatory gap" because they have related explanations.

"The binding problem" is similar to "the explanatory gap" problem in a couple of ways. First, is that it is a problem that also straddles the line between "the easy problems" and "the hard problem." The second is that the explanatory principles within Holoplexity are largely the same.

To begin, the structure of "the binding problem" is similar to that of "the explanatory gap." Similarly, the question is not *how* the background is perceived, not *how* objects are perceived, or not *how* emotional features occur; instead, the question is *why* those discrete stimuli are experienced as a singular experience.

Recall that it does not matter that the stimuli themselves differ in origin as exteroceptive or interoceptive; stimuli are stimuli. Recall that the COS is proposed to be actively embedded into *all* incoming stimuli. Recall further that the reflexive property of consciousness itself within the COS causes its experience of itself (COS) within the stimuli to be experienced as *not separate* or as *intimate*. This is an aspect of the "hard problem."

The question asks about how the discrete elements of an experience come to be experienced as a singular event. This aspect tends to be more in the domain of the "easy problems." Holoplexity theory is an additive theory in that it changes nothing about existing theory, but only tends to add to it—ideally with a plausible segue.

Part of the goal of this study was to create new theory in such a way that it leads to the doorstep of existing scientific thought.

Here, the question relates to the coming together of disparate elements of a singular experience. The segue here is to the doorstep of electromagnetically-based theories, such as Crick and Koch (1990). Crick and Koch provide a solution to the binding problem at the neurobiological level because they state there is a common neuronal oscillation (40 Hz) that binds together the relevant neural events (Tye, 2017). However, saying that "events" are "relevant" and thus bound together seems unsatisfactory as to *why* they are bound together.

Holoplexity theory suggests two additional theoretical reasons. First, are the rather mysterious (to me) properties of electromagnetic phenomena. The reflexive property of "consciousness itself" is presumed to extend to the electromagnetic. Meaning that it has a kind of attraction to itself as an aspect of its wholeness or oneness (holo-). Second, is the "dimension of consciousness itself" which is proposed to be "concurrently right here, right now—and everywhere, all the time." Recall that the primary dimension of "consciousness itself" is non-spatial and non-temporal. Recall further that each passing moment introduces some "change" into this dimension—meaning that in this dimension exists an exact "snapshot" (for lack of a better word) of one moment as the next moment is created by the introduction of some other "change." Thus, it is proposed that consciousness itself propagates reality as itself—to itself—via its own reflexive properties. The word "reality" here would be the "snapshot" and its inherent structure which is propagated through time—in reality, and thus phenomenally—since it has been established by reflexive monism (via perceptual projection) that they are one and the same.

Limitations

Broadly Conceptualized

Although this proposed theory was conceived at a broad conceptual level, it was designed to be compatible with empirical theories such as *Global Workspace Theories* (Baars, Dehaene) and *Information*

Integration Theory (Tononi). This is why the term *integration* was paired with the researcher's conceptualization of *unfolding*. These two terms are hardly synonymous alone but tend to point to the same general phenomenon within the proposed theory. The pairing was a literary mechanism intended to illustrate a conceptual parallel between the two theories.

Highly Speculative

As an original, empirically compatible, nonreductive theory of consciousness that offers a viable answer to the hard problem of consciousness, this proposed theory is highly speculative and contains hypotheses that have not achieved a high degree of general acceptance.

References

Anderson, S., Reznik, J., & Glassman, N. (2005). The unconscious relational self. In B. Hassin et. Al (Eds.), *The New Unconscious*. Cambridge, MA: MIT Press.

Atmanspacher, H. (2017). Quantum approaches to brain and mind. In S. Schneider & M. Velmans (Eds.), *The Blackwell Companion to Consciousness* (2nd ed., pp. 298-313). Hoboken, NJ: Wiley & Sons, Inc.

Baars, B. J. (2005). Global workspace theory of consciousness: Toward a cognitive neuroscience of human experience. *Progress in brain research. 150.* 45-53.

Baars. B. J. (2017). The global workspace theory of consciousness: Predictions and results. In S. Schneider & M. Velmans (Eds.), *The Blackwell Companion to Consciousness* (2nd ed., pp. 229-242). Hoboken, NJ: Wiley & Sons, Inc.

Bach-y-Rita, P., & Kercel, S. W. (2003). Sensory substitution and the human–machine interface. *Trends in cognitive sciences, 7*(12), 541-546.

Birks, M., & Mills, J. (2015). *Grounded theory: A practical guide.* Sage.

Blackmore, S. (2004). *Consciousness: An introduction.* New York: Oxford University Press.

Bloomberg, L. D. & Volpe, M. (2016). Completing your dissertation: A road map from beginning to end. In L. D. Bloomberg, L. D. *A complete dissertation: A big picture*, 3-12.

Bohm, D. (1980). *Wholeness and the implicate order*. New York: Routledge.

Bohm, D. & B. J. Hiley. (1993). *The undivided universe-an ontological interpretation of quantum mechanics*. New York: Routledge.

Carruthers, P. & Schecter, E. (2006). Can panpsychism bridge the explanatory gap? In A. Freeman (Ed.) (2006), *Consciousness and its place in nature: Does physicalism entail panpsychism?* (pp. 32-39). Exeter, UK: Imprint Academic.

Carruthers, P. (2017). Higher-order theories of consciousness. In S. Schneider & M. Velmans (Eds.), *The Blackwell Companion to Consciousness* (2nd ed., pp. 288-297). Hoboken, NJ: Wiley & Sons, Inc.

Carter, R. (2002). *Exploring Consciousness*. Los Angeles: University of California Press.

———. (2010). *Mapping the Mind*. Los Angeles: University of California Press.

———., Aldridge, S, Page, M., & Parker, S. (2014). *The Human Brain Book*. New York. DK Publishing.

Chalmers, D. J. (1995a). Facing up to the problem of consciousness. *Journal of Consciousness Studies 2*(3): 200-19.

———. (1995b). The Puzzle of Conscious Experience. *Scientific American, 273*(6), 80-86.

———. (1997). Moving forward on the problem of consciousness. *Journal of Consciousness Studies 4* (1): 3-46.

———. (1999). *The Conscious Mind: In Search of a Fundamental Theory.* New York: Oxford University Press.

———. (2017a). The hard problem of consciousness. In S. Schneider & M. Velmans (Eds.), *The Blackwell Companion to Consciousness* (2nd ed., pp. 32-42). Hoboken, NJ: Wiley & Sons, Inc.

———. (2017b). Naturalistic dualism. In S. Schneider & M. Velmans (Eds.), *The Blackwell Companion to Consciousness,* (2nd ed., pp. 363-373). Hoboken, NJ: Wiley & Sons, Inc.

———. (2018). The metaproblem of consciousness. *Journal of Consciousness Studies, 25*(9–10): 6–61.

Charmaz, K. 2000. Grounded theory: Objectivist and contructivist methods. In *The Handbook of Qualitative Research.* Edited by N. K. Denzin and Y. Lincoln. Thousand Oaks, CA: Sage.

Clark, A. (2005). *Situational Analysis: Grounded Theory After the Postmodern Turn.* Thousand Oaks, CA: Sage.

Coleman, S. (2006). Being realistic. In A. Freeman (Ed.) (2006), *Consciousness and its place in nature: Does physicalism entail panpsychism?* (pp. 40-52). Exeter, UK: Imprint Academic.

Corbin, J., & Strauss, A. (2008). *Basics of Qualitative Research: Techniques and Procedures for Developing Grounded Theory* (3rd ed.). Thousand Oaks, CA: Sage

Crick, F. & Koch, C. (1990) Towards a neurobiological theory of consciousness. *Seminars in the neurosciences, 2,* 263-275.

————. (2003). A framework for consciousness. *Nature Neuroscience, 6*, 119-126.

Damasio, A. R. (1996). The somatic marker hypothesis and the possible functions of the prefrontal cortex. Phil. Trans. R. Soc. Lond. B, 351(1346), 1413-1420.

————. (1999). *The Feeling of What Happens: Body and Emotion in the Making of Consciousness.* Orlando: Harcourt.

Dehaene, S. (2014). *Consciousness and the brain: deciphering how the brain codes our thoughts.* New York: Penguin Books.

Dennett, Daniel C. (1991). *Consciousness Explained.* New York: Little, Brown and Company.

Dretske, Fred (2012). Chris Hill's consciousness. *Philosophical Studies, 161*(3):497-502.

Eccles, J. C. (1994). *How the Self Controls Its Brain.* New York: Springer Verlag.

Edelman, G. M. & Tononi, G. (2000). *A Universe of Consciousness: How Matter Becomes Imagination.* New York: Basic Books.

Einstein, A. & Lawson, R. W. (1921). *Relativity: The special and general theory.* New York: Holt.

Freeman, A. (Ed.). (2006). *Consciousness and its place in nature: Does physicalism entail panpsychism?*. Exeter, UK: Imprint Academic.

Glaser, B. G. (1978). *Theoretical Sensitivity.* Sociology Press.

————. (2005). *The grounded theory perspective III: Theoretical Coding.* Mill Valley, CA: Sociology Press.

Goff, P. (2006). Experiences don't sum. In A. Freeman (Ed.) (2006), *Consciousness and its place in nature: Does physicalism entail panpsychism?* (pp. 53-61). Exeter, UK: Imprint Academic.

———. (2017). Panpsychism. In S. Schneider & M. Velmans (Eds.), *The Blackwell Companion to Consciousness* (2nd ed., pp. 106-124). Hoboken, NJ: Wiley & Sons, Inc.

Hallberg, L. R. M. (2010). Some Thoughts About the Literature Review in Ground Theory Studies. *Int J Qualitative Stud in Health Well-being, 5:5384.*

Hameroff, S. (2003). Time, consciousness and quantum events in fundamental spacetime geometry. In R. Buccheri, et al. (Eds.), *The Nature of Time: Geometry, Physics and Perception.* 77- 89.

———. & Penrose, R. (1996). Orchestrated Objective Reduction of Quantum Coherence in Brain Microtubules: The "Orch OR" Model for Consciousness. In *Toward a Science of Consciousness-The First Tucson Discussions and Debates.*

Hobson, J. A. (2017). States of consciousness: Waking, sleeping, and dreaming. In S. Schneider & M. Velmans (Eds.), *The Blackwell Companion to Consciousness* (2nd ed., pp. 127-140). Hoboken, NJ: Wiley & Sons, Inc.

Horgan, J. (2017). https://blogs.scientificamerican.com/cross-check/david-chalmers-thinks-the-hard-problem-is-really-hard/. (n.d.).

Jackson, F. (2006). Galen Strawson on panpsychism. In A. Freeman (Ed.) (2006), *Consciousness and its place in nature: Does physicalism entail panpsychism?* 62-64. Exeter, UK: Imprint Academic.

Klemm, W. R. (2011). Neural Representation of the Sense of Self. Archives Cognitive Psychology, *Advances in Cognitive Psychology, 7*: 16-30.

———. (2013). *Core ideas in Neuroscience* (2nd ed.).

———. (2014). *Mental biology: The new science of how the brain and mind relate.* New York: Prometheus Books.

———. (2019). *Triune brain, triune mind, triune worldview.* Mesa, AZ: Brighton Publishing, LLC.

Koch, C. (1992). What Is Consciousness? *Discover,* November; 96.

———., & Crick, F. (1994). CT Some Further Ideas Regarding the Neuronal Basis of Awareness. *Large-scale neuronal theories of the brain,* 93.

Kriegel, U. (2002). Panic theory and the prospectus for a representational theory of phenomenal consciousness. *Philosophical Psychology, 15*: 55-64.

Lamme, V. A. F. (2006). Towards a true neural stance on consciousness. *Trends in Cognitive Sciences, 10* (11): 494-501.

Lehar, S. (2003). *The world in your head.* Mahwah, NJ: Lawrence Erlbaum Associates, Inc.

Levine, J. (1983). Materialism and qualia: The explanatory gap. *Pacific philosophical quarterly, 64*(4), 354-361.

Libet, B. (1985). Unconscious cerebral initiative and the role of conscious will in voluntary action. *Behavioral and brain sciences, 8*(4), 529-539.

Lieberman, M. D., Jarcho, J. M., & Sapute, A. B. (2004). Evidence-based and intuition-based self-knowledge: An fMRI study. *Journal of Personality and Social Psychology, 87*(4), 421-435.

Lincoln, Y.S. & Guba, E.G. (1985). *Naturalistic Inquiry.* London: Sage.

Llinás, R. (2002). *I of the Vortex.* Westwood, MA: MIT Press.

London, F. & Bauer, E. (1939). The theory of observation in quantum mechanics. In Wheeler, J. A. & Zurek, W. H. (Eds.). (1983). *Quantum theory and measurement.* Princeton university press.

Lutz, A. (2007). Neurophenomenology and the study of self-consciousness. *Consciousness and cognition, 16*(3), 765-767.

Lycan, W. G. (2006). Resisting ?-ism. In A. Freeman (Ed.) (2006), *Consciousness and its place in nature: Does physicalism entail panpsychism?* (pp. 65-71). Exeter, UK: Imprint Academic.

Macpherson, F. (2006). Property dualism and the merits of solutions to the mind-body problem. In A. Freeman (Ed.) (2006), *Consciousness and its place in nature: Does physicalism entail panpsychism?* (pp. 72-89). Exeter, UK: Imprint Academic.

Martin, P. & Turner, B. (1986). Grounded Theory and Organizational Research. *The Journal of Applied Behavioral Science, 22*(2), 141-157.

Maxwell, G. (1978). *Rigid Designators and the Mind-Brain Identity.* Minneapolis: University of Minnesota Press.

McGinn, C. (1989). Can We Solve the Mind—Body Problem? *Mind, 98*(391), 349-366.

―――――. (1995). Consciousness and space. In Thomas Metzinger (ed.), *Journal of Consciousness Studies*. Imprint Academic. pp. 220-230.

―――――. (2006). Hard questions. In A. Freeman (Ed.) (2006), *Consciousness and its place in nature: Does physicalism entail panpsychism?* (pp. 90-99). Exeter, UK: Imprint Academic.

McGinn, C. (2011). *Basic Structures of Reality: Essays in Meta-Physics*. New York: Oxford University Press.

McGowan, P.O., Sasaki, A., Alesso, S., Dymov, S., Labonte, B., Szyf, G., & Meaney, M.J. (2009). *Epigenetic regulation of the glucocorticoid receptor in human brain associated with child abuse*. Nature Neuroscience, 12: 342-348.

Metzinger, T. (2009). *The ego tunnel: The science of the mind and the myth of the self.* New York: Basic Books.

―――――. (2013). Why are dreams interesting for philosophers? The example of minimal phenomenal selfhood, plus an agenda for future research. *Frontiers in Psychology, 4*: 746.

Neuman, W. L., & Kreuger, L. (2003). *Social work research methods: Qualitative and quantitative approaches*. Allyn and Bacon.

O'Regan, J. K., & Noë, A. (2001). A sensorimotor account of vision and visual consciousness. *Behavioral and Brain Sciences, 24*(5), 939-73.

Panksepp, J. (1998a). *Affective neuroscience: The foundations of human and animal emotions.* New York: Oxford University Press.

———. (1998b). The periconscious substrates of consciousness: Affective states and the evolutionary origins of the SELF. *Journal of Consciousness Studies, 5*, 566-582.

———. (2007a). The neuroevolutionary and neuroaffective psychobiology of the prosocial brain. In R. I. M. Dunbar & L. Barrett (Eds.), *The Oxford Handbook of Evolutionary Psychology* (pp. 145-162). Oxford: Oxford University Press.

———. (2007b). Affective Consciousness. In M. Velmans & S. Schneider (Eds.), *The Blackwell Companion to Consciousness* (pp. 114-129). Malden, MA: Blackwell Publishing.

———. & Northoff, G. (2009). The trans-species core SELF: The emergence of active cultural and neuro-ecological agents though self-related processing within subcortical-cortical midline networks. *Consciousness and Cognition, 18*, 193-215.

Papineau, D. (2006). Comments on Galen Strawson. In A. Freeman (Ed.) (2006), *Consciousness and its place in nature: Does physicalism entail panpsychism?* (pp. 100-109). Exeter, UK: Imprint Academic.

Reber, A. S., Allen, R., & Reber, E. S. (2009). *Penguin Dictionary of Psychology*. New York: Penguin Books.

Rees, G., & Frith, C. D. (2017). Methodologies for identifying the neural correlates of consciousness. In S. Schneider & M. Velmans (Eds.), *The Blackwell Companion to Consciousness* (2nd ed., pp. 589-606). Hoboken, NJ: Wiley & Sons, Inc.

Reichertz, J. (2007). Abduction: The logic of discovery of grounded theory. In A. Bryant and K. Charmaz (Eds.), *The Sage Handbook of Grounded Theory* (pp. 214-228). London: Sage.

Revonsuo, A. (2010). *Consciousness: The science of subjectivity.* New York: Psychology Press.

Rey, G. (2006). Better to study human than world psychology. In A. Freeman (Ed.) (2006), *Consciousness and its place in nature: Does physicalism entail panpsychism?* (pp. 110-116). Exeter, UK: Imprint Academic.

Rosenthal, D. M. (2004). Varieties of higher-order theory. In R. Gennaro (Ed.), *Higher-Order Theories of Consciousness*, 19-44. Philadelphia: John Benjamins.

————. (2006). Experience and the physical. In A. Freeman (Ed.) (2006), *Consciousness and its place in nature: Does physicalism entail panpsychism?* (pp. 117-128). Exeter, UK: Imprint Academic.

————. (2012). Higher-order awareness, misrepresentation, and function. Phil. Trans. R. Soc. Lond. B, 367 (1594), 1424-1438.

Prinz, J. J. (2017). The intermediate level theory of consciousness. In S. Schneider & M. Velmans (Eds.), *The Blackwell Companion to Consciousness* (2nd ed., pp. 257-268). Hoboken, NJ: Wiley & Sons, Inc.

Pylkkänen, P. T. (2006). *Mind, matter and the implicate order.* Springer Science & Business Media.

Schneider, S. & Velmans, M. (Eds.). (2017). *The Blackwell Companion to Consciousness* (2nd ed.). Hoboken, NJ: Wiley & Sons, Inc.

Schurger, A. (2017). The neuropsychology of conscious volition. In S. Schneider & M. Velmans (Eds.), *The Blackwell Companion to Consciousness* (2nd ed., pp. 695-710). Hoboken, NJ: Wiley & Sons, Inc.

Sherrington, C.S. (1906). *The integrative action of the nervous system.* New York: Charles Scribner's Sons.

Seager, W. (2006). The "intrinsic nature" argument for panpsychism. In A. Freeman (Ed.) (2006), *Consciousness and its place in nature: Does physicalism entail panpsychism?* (pp. 129-145). Exeter, UK: Imprint Academic.

————. & Bourget, D. (2017). Representationalism about consciousness. In S. Schneider & M. Velmans (Eds.), *The Blackwell Companion to Consciousness* (2nd ed., pp. 272-287). Hoboken, NJ: Wiley & Sons, Inc.

Searle, J. R. (1993). The Problem of Consciousness. *Social Research, 60*(1). 3–16.

————. (2000). Consciousness. *Annual Review of Neuroscience, 23*(1). 557.

————. (2017). Biological naturalism. In S. Schneider & M. Velmans (Eds.), *The Blackwell Companion to Consciousness,* (2nd ed., pp. 327-336). Hoboken, NJ: Wiley & Sons, Inc.

Shannon, C. E. (1948). A Mathematical Theory of Communication. *Bell Systems Technical Journal, 27*(3). 379-423.

Simons, P. (2006). The seeds of experience. In A. Freeman (Ed.) (2006), *Consciousness and its place in nature: Does physicalism entail panpsychism?* (pp. 146-150). Exeter, UK: Imprint Academic.

Singer, W. (2017). Consciousness processing: Unity in time rather than in space. In S. Schneider & M. Velmans (Eds.), *The Blackwell Companion to Consciousness,* (2nd ed., pp. 607-620). Hoboken, NJ: Wiley & Sons, Inc.

Skrbina, D. (2006). Realistic panpsychism. In A. Freeman (Ed.) (2006), *Consciousness and its place in nature: Does physicalism entail panpsychism?* (pp. 151-157). Exeter, UK: Imprint Academic.

Smart, J. J. C. (2006). Ockhamist comments on Strawson. In A. Freeman (Ed.) (2006), *Consciousness and its place in nature: Does physicalism entail panpsychism?* (pp. 158-162). Exeter, UK: Imprint Academic.

Stapp, H. P. (2006). Commentary on Strawson's target article. In A. Freeman (Ed.) (2006), *Consciousness and its place in nature: Does physicalism entail panpsychism?* (pp. 163-169). Exeter, UK: Imprint Academic.

Stoljar, D. (2006). Comments on Galen Strawson. In A. Freeman (Ed.) (2006), *Consciousness and its place in nature: Does physicalism entail panpsychism?* (pp. 170-176). Exeter, UK: Imprint Academic.

Strauss, A.L. & Corbin, J. M. (1990). *Basics of qualitative research: Grounded theory procedures and techniques.* Thousand Oaks, CA, US: Sage Publications, Inc.

————. (1998). *Basics of Qualitative Research: Techniques and Procedures for Developing Grounded Theory* (2nd ed.). Thousand Oaks, CA: Sage.

Strawson, G. (2006a). Why physicalism entails panpsychism. In A. Freeman (Ed.) (2006), *Consciousness and its place in nature: Does physicalism entail panpsychism?* (pp. 3-31). Exeter, UK: Imprint Academic.

————. (2006b). Panpsychism? Reply to commentators with a celebration of Descartes. In A. Freeman (Ed.) (2006), *Consciousness and its place in nature: Does physicalism entail panpsychism?* (pp. 184-280). Exeter, UK: Imprint Academic.

———. (2017). Physicalist panpsychism. In S. Schneider & M. Velmans (Eds.), *The Blackwell Companion to Consciousness* (2nd ed., pp. 374-390). Hoboken, NJ: Wiley & Sons, Inc.

Tononi, G. (2004). An information integration theory of consciousness. *BMC Neuroscience, 5*, 42 - 42.

———. (2017a). The information integrated theory of consciousness: An outline. In S. Schneider & M. Velmans (Eds.), *The Blackwell Companion to Consciousness* (2nd ed., pp. 243-256). Hoboken, NJ: Wiley & Sons, Inc.

———. (2017b). Integrated information theory of consciousness: Some ontological considerations. In S. Schneider & M. Velmans (Eds.), *The Blackwell Companion to Consciousness* (2nd ed.). Hoboken, NJ: Wiley & Sons, Inc.

Treisman, A. M., & Gelade, G. (1980). A feature-integration theory of attention. *Cognitive psychology, 12*(1), 97-136.

Trevarthen, C., & Aitken, K. (2001). Infant Intersubjectivity: Research, Theory, and Clinical Applications. The Journal of Child Psychology and Psychiatry and Allied Disciplines, 42(1), 3-48.

Tye, M. (2017). Philosophical problems of consciousness. In S. Schneider & M. Velmans (Eds.), *The Blackwell Companion to Consciousness* (2nd ed.). Hoboken, NJ: Wiley & Sons, Inc.

Varela, F. (1995). Neurophenomenology: A methodological remedy for the hard problem. *Journal of Consciousness Studies, 3*(4). 330-49.

Velmans, M. (1990). Consciousness, brain and the physical world. *Philosophical Psychology, 3*(1), 77.

————. (1999). Intersubjective science. *Journal of Consciousness Studies, 6*(2-3), 299-306.

————. (2008). Reflexive Monism. *Journal of Consciousness Studies, 15.* 5-50.

————. (2017a). Dualism, reductionism, and reflexive monism. In S. Schneider & M. Velmans (Eds.), *The Blackwell Companion to Consciousness* (2nd ed., pp. 349-362). Hoboken, NJ: Wiley & Sons, Inc.

————. (2017b). An epistemology for the study of consciousness. In S. Schneider & M. Velmans (Eds.), *The Blackwell Companion to Consciousness* (2nd ed., pp. 769-784). Hoboken, NJ: Wiley & Sons, Inc.

Vision, G. (2017). Emergentism. In S. Schneider & M. Velmans (Eds.), *The Blackwell Companion to Consciousness* (2nd ed., pp. 337-348). Hoboken, NJ: Wiley & Sons, Inc.

Voss, U., Holzmann, R., Tuin, I., & Hobson, A. (2009). Lucid Dreaming: A State of Consciousness with Features of Both Waking and Non-Lucid Dreaming. *Sleep 2009*; *32*(9): 1191-1200.

Ward, L. M. (2011). The thalamic dynamic core theory of conscious experience. *Consciousness and Cognition, 20*(2), 464–486.

Wheeler, J. A. (1990). Information, physics, quantum: The search for links. *Complexity, entropy, and the physics of information, 8.*

————., & Ford, K. W. (2000). *Geons, black holes, and quantum foam: a life in physics.* Norton.

————., & Zurek, W. H. (Eds.). (1983). *Quantum theory and measurement.* Princeton university press.

Wigner, E. P. (1961). Remarks on the mind-body question. In I. J. Good (Ed.) (1961), *Scientist Speculates.* New York: Basic Books.

Wilson, C. (2006). Commentary on Galen Strawson. In A. Freeman (Ed.) (2006), *Consciousness and its place in nature: Does physicalism entail panpsychism?* (pp. 177-183). Exeter, UK: Imprint Academic.

Zeki, S., & Bartels, A. (1999). Toward a theory of visual consciousness. *Consciousness and cognition, 8*(2), 225-259.

Index

A

Abduction, 12–13, 45, 49, 54–55, 95
Aldridge, 4, 70, 73, 83, 117
Amygdala, 13, 71, 86, 115
Apoptosis, 70, 114
Atmanspacher, 41, 46, 124
Audit trail, 57
Autopoiesis, 14, 43, 125
Awareness, 2, 7, 14, 19, 22, 31, 43, 65, 70, 73, 83, 106–107, 114–115, 117

B

Baars, 8, 37–38, 65–66, 136
Bach-y-Rita, 24, 30, 108–109
Back-action, 38
Bauer, 89
Big bang, 19, 42, 92–93, 100, 126
Binding problem, 14, 85, 110, 121, 128, 135–136
Biological naturalism, 6, 29, 31
Birks, 13, 19, 22–23, 50–51, 53, 56–58, 78, 86
Blackmore, 4, 31, 33, 36, 50, 73, 83, 117
Bloomberg, 78, 123
Bohm, 8, 38, 46, 65–66, 69, 76, 81–82, 103, 124, 126, 129, 132

Brain, 4, 6–8, 12–13, 15, 17–20, 23, 29, 33, 35–43, 45–46, 64–75, 77, 79–80, 83–86, 88, 90–92, 94, 98–99, 105–106, 108–109, 112–122, 127, 129–135

C

Capra, 72, 125
Carruthers, 5, 8, 29–31, 46, 63, 65–66, 71, 108–110, 116, 124
Carter, 4, 13, 50, 69–76, 83, 85–86, 115, 117–118, 128, 131
Central organizing mechanism, 15, 71, 76, 86, 115, 122, 132
Chalmers, 1, 3, 5, 8–10, 12, 17–18, 22, 31, 33, 37, 42, 46, 63, 65–66, 74, 79, 85–88, 97–99, 101–103, 105–107, 110, 112, 121, 124, 128, 133–134
Clark, 57
Coding, 13, 50–51, 54–56, 59–60, 62–63, 66–68, 86–87, 89, 121
Concept of self, 13–16, 19, 22–23, 32, 70–71, 76, 86, 114, 122, 127, 132
Consciousness, 1–12, 14–24, 26–56, 59–114, 116–137

Consciousness itself, 2, 4–9, 14–17, 19–20, 22, 24, 29, 32, 35, 37–43, 45–46, 54, 61, 65–74, 76–77, 79–82, 84–92, 94, 96, 100–114, 116–122, 124–127, 129–136
Constant comparative analysis, 12, 45, 49, 52–54, 59, 62, 92
Creswell, 11, 49
Crick, 6, 40, 64, 136

D

Damasio, 6, 36, 43, 64, 71, 116
Dehaene, 8, 38, 40, 65–66, 73, 83, 136
Dennett, 7–8, 33, 65, 117
Descartes, 1, 4, 102
Dimension, 5, 15, 20, 30, 35, 42, 54–56, 67–69, 72–74, 76–77, 79–85, 87, 90–93, 95–96, 99, 101–102, 104, 106–107, 109–114, 116, 118, 120–121, 124–125, 127, 129–131, 134, 136
Dretske, 7, 31, 65
Dual content, 108
Dualism, 4, 8, 18, 33, 46, 66, 83, 102, 105–106, 124
Dynamic core, 6, 37, 39–40, 44, 116

E

Easy problems, 3, 5, 9, 14, 16–17, 22, 42, 63–64, 86, 116, 132–135
Eccles, 5, 41, 46, 63, 124
Edelman, 4, 6, 37, 39–40, 44, 64, 116

Electromagnetism, 16, 91–92, 121
Emergentism, 7, 16, 30, 52–54, 65, 89
Empiricism, 51, 62
Epiphenomenalism, 17, 29, 41, 99, 131
Epistemology, 17, 48
Explanatory gap, 9, 17, 19, 22, 32, 85, 103, 110, 115, 121, 128, 132–133, 135
Extra ingredient, 8–9, 17, 22, 33, 42, 66, 77, 85, 88, 103, 112, 128, 130–131

F

It from bit, 82, 96
Functionalism, 7, 65, 103

G

Glaser, 27, 50, 52, 88
Global workspace, 8, 37–38, 46, 66, 136
Grounded theory, 11–13, 21–23, 25, 27–28, 44, 48–60, 78–79, 86–89, 122

H

Hallberg, 27
Hameroff, 5–6, 41, 46, 63–64, 69, 94, 124–125
Hard problem, 1, 3, 6–12, 16–19, 21–22, 24, 27–28, 32, 36–37, 40, 42, 45, 48–52, 60, 63–67, 78–79, 87–88, 93, 99, 106, 116, 123–124, 127, 132, 135, 137

Heisenberg, 68, 89, 103
Hippocampus, 13, 18, 71, 86, 115
Holomovement, 38, 82, 126, 129, 134
Holoplexity, 2, 4, 6, 8, 10, 12–16, 18, 20–22, 24, 26, 28, 30, 32, 34, 36, 38, 40, 42, 44, 46, 50, 52, 54, 56, 58, 60, 62, 64, 66, 68, 70, 72–74, 76–77, 79–82, 84, 86, 88–90, 92, 94–96, 98, 100, 102–114, 116, 118–124, 126, 128–136
Human Consciousness, 1–2, 4, 6–9, 14–17, 19, 22–23, 28–29, 32–34, 37–39, 42–43, 45–46, 65–68, 72–74, 79–80, 83–84, 87–91, 94, 98, 101, 106–107, 110, 113, 117, 121–122, 124–127

I

Implicate order, 8, 38, 46, 66, 124
Induction, 19, 54
Information integration, 8, 37, 39, 42–44, 66, 119–121
Intermediate level, 7

J

Jackendoff, 39

K

Kant, 5
Kercel, 24, 30, 108–109
Klemm, 36, 69–73, 75–76, 83, 116–117, 132
Koch, 6, 40, 64, 136

Kriegel, 116
Kripke, 133

L

Lamme, 5, 7, 42, 63, 65
Lehar, 7, 36, 65
Levine, 9, 17, 22, 85, 103, 110, 115, 121, 128, 132–133
Llinas, 6, 42, 44, 64
London, 89
Luisi, 125

M

Maturana, 14, 43, 46, 124–125
McGinn, 42, 46, 74, 81, 85, 92, 94–95, 100–101, 104–105, 112–113, 124, 128–129
Memos, 50, 57–58
Metzinger, 7, 36, 65
Microconsciousness, 7, 40, 46, 65, 124
Mills, 13, 19, 22–23, 50–51, 53, 56–58, 78, 86
Monism, 4, 8, 21, 35, 46, 57, 66, 74, 79, 100, 110–112, 120, 124, 136
Multiple drafts, 7, 33, 38, 117
Multiplicity, 18, 79, 81–82, 90, 92, 96–97, 101–102

N

Naturalistic dualism, 8, 33, 46, 66, 102, 106, 124
Neurobiological, 6, 40, 116, 136

Neurocognitive, 14–15, 19–20, 22–23, 44, 70–73, 75–77, 86, 114–116, 121, 130, 132
Neurophenomenology, 7, 34, 46, 65
New explanatory bridging principle, 73, 85, 128, 131
Noe, 6–7, 34, 36, 64–65
Nonlocality, 20

O

Ontology, 8, 16, 20, 35, 48, 65–66, 99, 108
O'Regan, 6–7, 34, 36, 64–65
Organizational invariance, 10, 107

P

Page, 4, 70, 73, 83, 95, 117
Panpsychism, 8, 20, 23, 30, 34, 40, 46, 52–55, 66, 80, 83, 89, 95–96, 124–127
Parker, 4, 70, 73, 83, 117
Penrose, 5–6, 41, 46, 63–64, 124
Perceptual projection, 20–22, 35, 75–76, 112, 120–121, 128–129, 136
Physicalist panpsychism, 8, 34, 46, 66, 124
Prinz, 5, 7, 39–40, 63, 65
Pylkkanen, 76, 132

Q

Quantum, 6, 8, 20–21, 38, 41, 46, 61, 64, 74, 81–82, 92, 98, 103, 124–126, 129, 132, 134
Quantum foam, 82, 126, 129

R

Recurrent processing, 7, 42, 65
Recursive, 21, 52, 73, 76, 79, 89
Reflexive, 8, 21, 35, 43, 46, 57, 66, 74, 100, 110–112, 116, 120, 124, 126–127, 129–131, 135–136
Representationalism, 6, 32, 34, 46, 64
Revonsuo, 4, 20, 29, 33, 39, 50, 70
Rosenthal, 7–8, 31, 46, 65, 124

S

Santiago theory, 14, 36, 43, 46, 124–125
Sarfatti, 38, 76, 132
Schneider, 50
Schrodinger, 68, 89
Seager, 5–6, 32, 34, 46, 63–64, 116
Searle, 6, 29, 31
Self-awareness, 70, 73, 114
Sensorimotor, 7, 34, 36, 65
Sentience, 13–14, 16, 20, 22–23, 70, 114, 131–132
Sherrington, 69, 73
Singer, 69, 73
Somatic marker, 6, 43

Space, 2, 30, 35, 40, 42–43, 55,
   72–73, 83, 85, 95, 97, 100–101,
   104, 107, 109, 117, 128–129
Storyline technique, 56, 60, 62,
   87, 122
Strauss, 52, 56, 88
Strawson, 5, 8, 29, 34, 46, 63,
   65–66, 95, 124
Substantive codes, 22, 57

T

Temporary sentience acquisition
   system, 13, 16, 23, 70, 114, 131
Thalamocortical binding, 6, 44
Theoretical integration, 23, 54,
   56, 60, 62, 86–87
Theoretical saturation, 23, 55
Theory, 1–18, 20–66, 68, 70–82,
   84–90, 92–137
Time, 2, 5, 19, 23, 35, 40–41, 47,
   50, 53–56, 61, 68–69, 71, 73,
   75–76, 80–81, 83–87, 90, 92–
   94, 96, 99, 102, 104, 107–108,
   110–113, 115, 117–118, 120–
   122, 124–127, 130, 134, 136
Tononi, 4–6, 8, 37, 39–40, 42–44,
   64, 66, 116, 119–120, 137
Treisman, 14, 85, 110, 128
Tye, 14, 136

U

Unfolding, 24, 76, 84–85, 90–91,
   101, 109–110, 118–121, 133,
   137

V

Varela, 5–7, 14, 34, 43, 46, 63–
   65, 124–125
Velmans, 8, 21–22, 35, 46, 50,
   57, 66, 74–75, 85, 100, 110,
   112, 116, 120, 124, 128–130
Virtual reality theory, 36
Vision, 7, 30–31, 65, 72, 91, 100,
   108, 110, 117–118, 133–134
In vivo codes, 19, 22, 51, 56, 62
Volpe, 78, 123

W

Wheeler, 79, 81–82, 89, 93, 96,
   105, 126, 129
Wigner, 90

Z

Zeki, 5–7, 40, 46, 63–65, 69, 124
Zurek, 90

GCRR PRESS

INTERNATIONAL DISTRIBUTION

39,000 online and in-store outlets like Amazon, Walmart, Target, and Barnes & Noble

EXPANDED ADVERTISING

Developed with search optimization technology, we offer an expanded Advertising package that involves delivery of your book to one of the industry's largest book distributors, as well as circulating information about the book to 7,000 top U.S. booksellers and librarians, as well as to over 27,000 international and domestic customers with more than 150,000 monthly views and 70,000 registered users.

HIGHER AUTHOR ROYALTIES!